PLANT-BASED DIET MEAL PLAN

A complete four-week plan to kick-start your healthy, slow and permanent weight loss. Vegan meal prep with tasty plant-based wholefood recipes and shopping list

Julie T. Evans

© **Copyright 2020 - All rights reserved.**

The content contained within this book may not be reproduced, duplicated or transmitted without direct written permission from the author or the publisher.

Under no circumstances will any blame or legal responsibility be held against the publisher, or author, for any damages, reparation, or monetary loss due to the information contained within this book. Either directly or indirectly.

Legal Notice:

This book is copyright protected. This book is only for personal use. You cannot amend, distribute, sell, use, quote or paraphrase any part, or the content within this book, without the consent of the author or publisher.

Disclaimer Notice:

Please note the information contained within this document is for educational and entertainment purposes only. All effort has been executed to present accurate, up to date, and reliable, complete information. No warranties of any kind are declared or implied. Readers acknowledge that the author is not engaging in the rendering of legal, financial, medical or professional advice. The content within this book has been derived from various sources. Please consult a licensed professional before attempting any techniques outlined in this book.

By reading this document, the reader agrees that under no circumstances is the author responsible for any losses, direct or indirect, which are incurred as a result of the use of information contained within this document, including, but not limited to errors, omissions, or inaccuracies.

Table of Contents

Introduction 8

The principles and benefits of plant-based diet. 9

    Transitioning into a plant-based lifestyle 10

    Benefits of Plant-Based Diet 10

Daily caloric intake for men and women 13

    Protein 14

    Fats 16

    Omega 3-6-9 17

    Carbs 17

    Micronutrient Intake 18

    Daily Needs of Micronutrients 18

    Eating healthy and losing weight 20

    Macros 21

Simple physical activity to help weight loss 22

    How does yoga benefit women? 22

    Weight Loss Benefits of Yoga 23

    Select suitable sports to change your physique 25

    Simple Sleep Truth 28

Four-week meal plan recipes 29

    DAY 1 30

        Breakfast: Orange French toast 30

        Lunch: Coconut Cauliflower Curry 31

        Dinner: Dinnertime Vegetable Soup 32

        Snack: Roasted Chickpeas 33

    DAY 2 34

        Breakfast: Chocolate Chip Coconut Pancakes 34

        Lunch: Healthy Green Soup 35

        Dinner: Tacos with Salsa 36

        Snack: Gluten-Free Pistachios 37

    DAY 3 38

        Breakfast: Eggless Scrambles 38

        Lunch: Simple Veggies Stew 39

        Dinner: Green Gram Split Lentil Recipe 40

        Snack: Cauliflower Poppers with Sauce 41

    DAY 4 42

        Breakfast: Breakfast Blueberries Pancakes 42

        Lunch: Garlic Pasta 43

- Dinner: Roasted Cauliflower Soup — 44
- Snack: Banana-Oat Protein Balls — 45

DAY 5 — 46
- Breakfast: Panini Recipe — 46
- Lunch: Quinoa Lime Burrito Bowl — 47
- Dinner: Rosemary Balsamic Roasted Vegetable — 48
- Snack: Dark Chocolate Figs — 49

DAY 6 — 50
- Breakfast: Mushroom, Olives and Chickpea Omelette — 50
- Lunch Tomato Soup — 51
- Dinner: Instant Pot Acorn Squash with Cranberries — 52
- Snack: Herb-Crusted Asparagus Spears — 53

DAY 7 — 54
- Breakfast: Whole-Wheat Berry Muffins — 54
- Lunch: Chickpea Cauliflower Quiche — 55
- Dinner: Indian Peanut Noodles — 56
- Snack: Peanut Butter and Chocolate Bars — 57

DAY 8 — 58
- Breakfast: Mason Jar Overnight Oats — 58
- Lunch: Cold Raw Peanut Soup — 59
- Dinner: Zucchini with Stuffing — 60
- Snack: Carrot Cake Oatmeal — 61

DAY 9 — 62
- Breakfast: Oats Pancakes — 62
- Lunch: Avocado Toast — 63
- Dinner: Tofu and Peanut Satay — 64
- Snack: No Bake Oatmeal Bars — 65

DAY 10 — 66
- Breakfast: Triple Berry Porridge — 66
- Lunch: Tofu Tikka Masala in Instant Pot — 67
- Dinner: Simple Spinach Soup — 68
- Snack: Strawberries Popsicles — 69

DAY 11 — 70
- Breakfast: Keto Cinnamon Coffee — 70
- Lunch: Baked Veggies with Sauce — 71
- Dinner: Coconut Cabbage Stew — 72
- Dessert: Fat Bombs — 73

DAY 12 — 74
- Breakfast: Savory Cauliflower Bread — 74
- Lunch: Pasta Salad — 75
- Dinner: Zucchini-Mushroom Bowl — 76
- Snack: Herbed Potato Hummus — 77

DAY 13 — 78
- Breakfast: Raspberry Truffle Brownies — 78
- Lunch: Broccoli Lemon Pasta — 79
- Dinner: Sweet Potato Soup — 80
- Snack: Raw Broccoli Poppers — 81

DAY 14 — 82
- Breakfast: Lemon Muffins — 82
- Lunch: Tofu Chow Mein — 83

- Dinner: Vegan Tacos 84
- Snack: Strawberry-Mango Ice 85

DAY 15 86
- Breakfast: Zucchini bread with pistachios and fennel 86
- Lunch: Cashew Siam Salad 87
- Dinner: Chickpea, Mango and Curried Cauliflower Salad 88
- Dessert: Double Chocolate Cupcakes 89

DAY 16 90
- Breakfast: Zucchini quinoa peas pancakes 90
- Lunch: Butternut Squash Tacos with Tempeh Chorizo 91
- Dinner: Healthy Lentil Soup 92
- Dessert: Lemony Oats Cookies 93

DAY 17 94
- Breakfast: Banana chocolate chip muffins 94
- Lunch: Avocado and Cauliflower Hummus 95
- Dinner: Roasted Vegetables and Lentil Salad 96
- Dessert: Raspberry Brownies 97

DAY 18 98
- Breakfast: Cardamom persimmon scones with maple cream 98
- Lunch: Raw Zoodles with Avocado 'N Nuts 99
- Dinner: Spicy SunDried Tomato Soup with White Beans & Swiss Chard 100
- Dessert: Plant-Based Mug Cake 101

DAY 19 102
- Breakfast: Quinoa crepes 102
- Lunch: Spicy Black Bean Soup 103
- Dinner: Cauliflower Sushi 104
- Dessert: Quinoa Pudding 105

DAY 20 106
- Breakfast: Coconut brown rice dressed in avocado cream 106
- Lunch: Spinach and Mashed Tofu Salad 107
- Dinner: Black Bean and Corn Salad 108
- Dessert: Cherry Soft-Serve Ice Cream 109

DAY 21 110
- Breakfast: Buckwheat and coconut porridge with blueberry sauce 110
- Lunch: Cucumber Edamame Salad 111
- Dinner: Tempeh Burgers 112
- Dessert: Pumpkin Oatmeal Muffins 113

DAY 22 114
- Breakfast: Buckwheat and hempseed pancakes 114
- Lunch: Artichoke White Bean Sandwich Spread 115
- Dinner: Edamame Salad 116
- Dessert: Easy Brownies 117

DAY 23 118
- Breakfast: Protein pancakes 118
- Lunch: Buffalo Chickpea Wraps 119
- Dinner: Zucchini Sandwich with Balsamic Dressing 120
- Dessert: Homemade Chocolate Ice-Cream 121

DAY 24 122
- Breakfast: Quinoa and oats focaccia bread 122
- Lunch: Coconut Veggie Wraps 123

  Dinner: Delicious Sloppy Joes With No Meat _____ 124
  Dessert: Dessert Time Parfait _____ 125
 DAY 25 _____ 126
  Breakfast: Sweet molasses bread _____ 126
  Lunch: Cucumber Avocado Sandwich _____ 127
  Dinner: Ricotta Basil Pinwheels _____ 128
  Dessert: Applesauce Muffins _____ 129
 DAY 26 _____ 130
  Breakfast: Chocolate Peanut Butter Shake _____ 130
  Lunch: Lentil Sandwich Spread _____ 131
  Dinner: Sweet Potato Sandwich Spread _____ 132
  Dessert: Keto Vanilla Pannacotta _____ 133
 DAY 27 _____ 134
  Breakfast: Berries Smoothie _____ 134
  Lunch: Rice and Bean Burritos _____ 135
  Dinner: Mediterranean Tortilla Pinwheels _____ 136
  Dessert: Apple Pie Bites _____ 137
 DAY 28 _____ 138
  Breakfast: Sunrise Smoothie _____ 138
  Lunch: Sun-dried Tomato Spread _____ 139
  Dinner: Spicy Hummus and Apple Wrap _____ 140
  Dessert: Cinnamon Spiced Apples _____ 141

Shopping list _____ 142

Week 1: Shopping List _____ 142

Week 2: Shopping List _____ 143

Week 3: Shopping List _____ 144

Week 4: Shopping List _____ 145

Conclusion _____ 147

By the same author _____ 147

Introduction

With this cookbook, you will enjoy simple and delicious plant-based diet meals that you will love and eat again!

While starting a diet can be challenging enough, it is even harder trying to stick with it when life is coming at you from all different directions. Whether you are dealing with a partner, child, or job responsibility, it is all too easy to put our diets in the back seat!

If you are sick and tired of feeling like junk because you are eating junk, now is the time to make a change! While it may seem like work at first, you have come to the right place to help you get started! Within the chapters of this book, you will be handed everything you need to help you with your new health journey.

When you first begin a plant-based diet, there will be many who question your choices. What many people don't understand is that eating a plant-based diet is natural and our bodies are meant to run on clean energy that plant-based foods provide. Before you know it, you will be losing weight and feeling healthier than ever before.

It is going to take some practice, but it all comes down to creating healthier habits. As you learn the foods, you will be able to enjoy a plant-based diet; it will be easier for you to follow. If you believe in yourself and put in the hard work, you can accomplish anything!

The principles and benefits of plant-based diet.

Whole foods and plant based diet are sometimes called WFPB diet; even though many dieticians and doctors have certain disparities on the lists of what plant based diets are, they all agree on one thing: plant based diet or WFPB is more than a diet. *Above all things, it is a lifestyle.*

It is a lifestyle which means different things for different people because individuals also determine what the plant based diet is to them. While some people give room for animal products such as eggs and milk, others decide not to allow any form of animal products in their diet. However, most people plant based diet has certain qualities that make them generally acceptable to dieticians, doctors and individuals. These qualities are:

-The food only is basically plants such as veggies, fruits, legumes, seeds, whole grains and nuts

-There is a reduction or total ban on animal based products (depending on the individual)

-This diet helps you to focus on the quality of the food you consume and many of the plant based diet proponents are hundred percent organic foods and they are locally sourced.

-All plant based diet foods are whole with no processing (or very little processing if any)

These basic reasons are the reasons why this diet is sometimes mistaken as vegan or vegetarian diet, even though they have their similarities the still have their peculiarities.

So what's the difference?

<u>Vegan diet</u>: People who stick with vegan diets stay away from all forms of animal products such as seafood, honey, meat, eggs, milk and poultry.

<u>Vegetarians</u>: There are two types of vegetarians: there are those who eat dairy, seafood and eggs. There are also vegetarians who remove poultry and meat from their diet.

<u>Plant-based diet</u>: The plant based diet is rather flexible. Many of the followers consume purely plant based foods but animal products aren't a life-threatening taboo (even though some people see it that way). Some people stick to a thorough plant-based diet only while others consume milk, eggs poultry, meat and seafood. Plant based diet or plant forward diet (as it is called by some people) are diets that make you focus on healthy foods from plant based sources.

Are plant based diets the way to go?

Some people have had reason to ask me if plant based diets are really the way to go because there are also health benefits that can be derived from other sources that aren't purely plant based.

True, but then you have nothing to lose when you stick with a pure plant based diet. With a plant based diet, you get the necessary nutrients such as vitamins, fats, proteins, minerals and carbohydrates for a healthy diet and body and they are rich in phytonutrients and fiber. For those who leave out all forms of animal products from their diet, you will need to take some food nutrients like B12 so your body can get all the nutrients it needs.

Some people have told me I would have gone for this diet but my options are limited.

There is no greater lie than this. Do you know you can make smoothies, purees, pizzas and other mouth-watering and delicious dishes that leave your taste buds craving for more; plus they are all healthy and nutritious plant based foods! You can't have it any better.

Even though you stick with this diet, you can be sure that you have all the required nutrients in your food even though it is a plant based diet. Plant based foods makes sure your body doesn't lack any minerals that it is required for the healthy development and growth of the body.

Transitioning into a plant-based lifestyle

I know you may be scared or worried about this lifestyle and how you have to let go of the meatballs and the other delicious meals you are used to but then I want to remind you of something; you grew up to become the person you are now. Your body and your mind changed overtime and you adjusted to these changes.

In the same way, I prefer a gradual change so your body can ease into this lifestyle. It is one step at a time until your body is fully settled into this lifestyle without stress and sweats.

Easy does it! You will get to love this diet and make it a lifestyle in no time so be calm about it; there's no need to rush it.

Benefits of Plant-Based Diet

There are many benefits to follow this diet mainly overall increase in wellness and being less sick. The concept has been around for a long time that increasing consumption of plant-derived foods makes the person more active and healthier. These people also seem to be happier and less irritated which makes life easier and far more relaxing. There are other advantages which come with the diet. Some of them are listed below:

-There's no need to count calories in this diet. It can be a tedious and time-wasting task that a busy person cannot afford. This diet simply allows some food and restricts the rest. A calorie doesn't tell much about the food, what nutrients are in it or is it healthy or not.

-It is a good way to lose weight. A recent 2018 control experiment showed that people that follow a vegan diet rather than those who eat meat, were more likely to lose weight. The study followed obese participants following normal diets and some following vegan diets and the result was that dieters almost lost 15 pounds in 4 months.

-Plant-based foods are full of carbs and fiber which fills up the stomach quickly making you feel less hungry. You will consume less of the foods that will be no good for you like sodas or candies. Cravings will not hit you as hard as if you were hungry.

--There is a higher quantity of water in plant-based food which increases body metabolism and reduces appetite. Water has many benefits, being hydrated makes you have better hair, skin and makes you look fresh.

Eating mostly plant-based foods increases mortality by preventing life long diseases. A recent 2019 study done by the American Heart Association showed that plant-eaters were less likely to develop heart diseases. It is also linked with lowering the chances of stroke, diabetes type 2, hypertension, and obesity.

It also has shown to increase insulin sensitivity in diabetic patients. In the 2009 study, over tens of thousands of participants were approached and the percentage of vegans developing diabetes was found to be 2.9% less than others. A review published in 2018 stated that diabetes is improved when following any diet that increases plant content.

By following this diet, you will not only help yourself in becoming better but also push the environment to progress in the right direction. A lot of pollutants come from beef and poultry farms. Making meat puts high stress on our planet and by consuming less of it, you are leaving less of a carbon footprint. Also by this diet, you are discouraging the use of meat as well.

It doesn't require any sort of investment and a person can begin it as soon as they decide to. Plant-based products are everywhere and even in a normal diet, take up a big portion of it. Some dieting programs and fads take a lot of money from people giving only temporary results but this diet has shown to reduce the most amount of weight. For some people starting this diet can be hard but if you want to reach your weight loss goals or become generally more fit than this diet is suited for you.

Many people practice this lifestyle for various reasons. From spending many years as a coach, I have come to discover from speaking with people who have tried and are still on this lifestyle that being on the whole foods plant based diet has really being of huge benefits to them.

Weight Loss and Weight Management: Sticking with a whole foods and plant based diet can reduce the pressure we face from losing weight. When you decide to lose weight, you're simply trying to lose more calories than consume. Calories are what the body uses as a source for fuel and it burns it to become energy that can be used.

Disease Prevention: Plant based diets are rich in fruits, vegetables, legumes, whole grains, nuts and seeds. It is a wonderful way to achieve great health and a healthy lifestyle. These foods are free from cholesterol, high in fiber, rich in vitamins, minerals and free from all forms of saturated fat.

Eating from a wide range of plant based diets provides the body with the protein, calcium, vitamins, minerals and other important nutrients it needs. Some of the meals taken from a Whole Foods Plant Based Diet are high antioxidants, vitamins, iron, calcium, iodine, Omega3 Fatty acids, and many other healthy essential nutrients.

Improves Digestion: Plant based diet improves digestion due to its fiber content. Plants are full of fiber and fiber is paramount to good digestion because fiber doesn't get broken down by our digestive enzymes so it has to go through the gastrointestinal tract without absorption. There are different types of fiber. Soluble fiber (it is called soluble fiber because it dissolves when it is in water) is a healthy fiber which slows the digestion process and aids nutrient absorption from foods. It also helps the gut microbes as the bacteria in the gut can munch on it. This is what is found in foods like vegetables, peas, beans, fruits and psyllium seed based fiber supplements.

Get Healthy Skin, Hair and Nails. Many followers claim to have seen tremendous changes in their skin, hair and nails. Dry and cracked skins tend to give way to a smooth and moisturized looking skin, same also for nails and hair. By eating foods with a variety of colors (different kinds of vegetables with colors) and a wide range of plant based foods, your body will be able to absorb nutrients, fiber, mineral and vitamins.

Greener Environment. Another benefit of this diet is that as it helps you, it is also helping the environment and our planet at large. This helps in reducing water consumption and land used for factories, greenhouse gas emissions, which are factors in environmental degradation and global warming.

This is a diet that can be at every age and life-stage, and also at any location. There are studies that show that fruit and vegetable diet have lower environmental impact. This is because you need to eat more plant products to substitute the animal produce you cut out of your diet.

Daily caloric intake for men and women

When preparing your meals, you will need to calculate their macronutrient breakdown and how many calories each meal contains. The included meal-plan provides this already if you choose to follow or pick days to eat from the 30-day meal plan.

To benefit from this process, you need to know how much you need to eat each day. That's why daily caloric needs, also known as basal metabolic rate, is essential for keeping track of your daily macro intake. How to calculate your specific needs is explained in the following paragraph.

This is the formula you need to use to calculate basal metabolic rate (BMR):

Ø Men: BMR = (9.99 x weight in kilograms) + (6.25 x height in centimeters) - 4.92 x age in years + 5.

Ø Women: BMR = (9.99 x weight in kilograms) + (6.25 x height in centimeters) - (4.92 x age in years) - 161.

Ø Multiply the BMR number with the activity factor that fits your lifestyle. With no exercise, your activity factor is 1.2. Exercise one to three times a week and your activity factor is 1.375. If you engage in exercise three to five times per week, the activity factor is 1.55. For heavy exercise, six to seven times a week, the activity factor is 1.725 and in case of an athlete or heavy training sessions and/or having a physically demanding job, your activity factor is 1.9. The number derived from this second calculation is the number of calories (kcal) required for maintaining a healthy weight.

Lowering your carb and fat intakes will allow you to burn fat more efficiently.

For people that pursue a fit lifestyle, a carb to protein to fat intake ratio of 50:25:25 is ideal.

Once you have achieved your goals and wish to simply maintain your body weight, you need to focus on stabilizing your caloric intake with at least 15-20% of your calories coming from protein.

The following is a breakdown of how to achieve the 50:25:25 ratio on a 2000-calorie diet:

• 50% carbohydrates: 2000 x 50% = 1000 calories per day. To determine the grams needed, divide 1000 by 4 to get 250 grams of carbohydrates required on a daily basis.

• 25% protein: 2000 x 25% = 500 calories per day. Divide 500 calories by 4 to get 125 g of protein needed on a daily basis.

• 25% fat: 2000 x 25% = 500 calories per day. Divide 500 calories by 9 to get ~55.6 g of fat needed on a daily basis.

Protein

Protein is vital to the proper functioning of all living things. The basic molecules that make up proteins are amino acids, also known as "the building blocks of life".

Amino acids compose many of the body's structures including nails, muscle, skin and hair. Some sources of vegan protein include tempeh, beans, quinoa, lentils, raw arugula, russet potatoes, raw collard greens, raw broccoli, raw spinach, boiled water chestnuts, boiled artichokes, boiled sweet corn and raw kale.

The table below shows the protein sources and their macronutrient breakdowns:

Food	Serving	Metric	Fats(g)	Carbs(g)	Fiber(g)	Protein(g)	Net Carbs(g)
Edamame	100g	100g	9	8.4	6	18.2	2.4
Lentils	100g	100g	0.4	20.1	7.9	9	12.2
White Beans	100g	100g	0.4	25.1	6.3	9.7	18.8
Cranberry Beans	100g	100g	0.5	24.5	8.6	9.3	15.9
Split Peas	100g	100g	0.4	21.1	8.3	8.3	12.8
Pinto Beans	100g	100g	0.7	26.2	9	9	17.2
Kidney Beans	100g	100g	0.5	22.8	6.4	8.7	16.4
Black Beans	100g	100g	0.5	23.7	8.7	8.9	15
Navy Beans	100g	100g	0.6	26.1	10.5	8.2	15.6
Lima Beans	100g	100g	0.3	23.6	5.4	6.8	18.2
Cornmeal (Grits)	100g	100g	3.6	76.9	7.3	8.1	69.6
Kamut	100g	100g	0.8	27.6	4.3	5.7	23.3
Teff, cooked	100g	100g	0.7	19.9	2.8	3.9	17.1
Quinoa	100g	100g	1.9	21.3	2.8	4.4	18.5

Couscous, cooked	1 oz.	86g	0.1	20	1.2	3.3	18.8
Oatmeal	100g	100g	1.5	12	1.7	2.5	10.3
Buckwheat Groats	100g	100g	0.6	19.9	2.7	3.4	17.2
Millet	100g	100g	1	23.7	1.3	3.5	22.4
Artichokes	100g	100g	0.2	10.5	5.4	10.5	5.1
Green Peas	100g	100g	0.2	15.6	5.5	5.4	10.1
Soybean Sprouts	½ cup	35g	2.3	3.3	0.4	4.6	3
Yellow Corn Sweet	100g	100g	1.4	18.7	2	3.3	16.7
Brussels Sprouts	½ cup	78g	0.4	5.5	2	2	3.5
Button Mushrooms	100g	100g	0.3	4	1.8	3.6	2.2
Broccoli	½ cup	78g	0.3	5.6	2.6	1.9	3
Guavas	100g	100g	1	14.3	5.4	2.6	8.9
Apricots	100g	100g	0.4	11.1	2	1.4	9.1
Kiwifruit	100g	100g	0.5	14.7	3	1.1	11.7
Blackberries	100g	100g	0.5	9.6	5.3	1.4	4.3
Oranges	100g	100g	0.1	11.8	2.4	0.9	9.4
Cantaloupe Melons	100g	100g	0.2	8.2	0.9	0.8	7.3
Hemp Seed	1 oz.	28g	13.8	2.5	1.1	9	1.3
Pumpkin Seeds	1 oz.	28g	13.9	4.2	1.8	8.5	2.3
Peanuts	1 oz.	28g	14.1	6	2.4	6	3.7
Pistachio Nuts	1 oz.	28g	13	8	2.9	6	5.1
Sunflower Seeds	1 oz.	28g	14.1	4.3	2.6	5.5	1.8

Pine Nuts	1 oz.	28g	19.4	3.7	1.1	3.9	2.7
Chickpeas	1 cup	164g	4.2	45	12.5	14.5	7.9
Amaranth	1 cup	28g	0.1	1.1	0	0.1	1.1

Amino acids are also involved in many of the body's chemical reactions, as they are the basic components of enzymatic structures and other chemical molecules. This ultimately means that they regulate mood, growth, and tissue repair, as they control the buildup and breakdown of complex molecules.

A couple of exceptional plant foods are soy and quinoa, which contain a great balance of amino acids. Soy contains all nine essential amino acids, making it a complete protein source.

Fats

Over the past three decades, it has been drilled into our minds that fats are bad. Period. However, the truth of the matter is that the body needs fats. For one, we need fat to absorb certain fat-soluble vitamins like A, D, E and K. Without fat, the body is not able to absorb those much-needed vitamins. Additionally, we need fat for healthy skin and hair as well as a protective insulator.

Your body is unable to produce essential fatty acids, so it is critical that you consume good fat sources. These essential fats help with numerous body processes like regulating blood pressure, protecting organs and brain development functions.

Consuming unsaturated fats is your best bet. Unsaturated fats are in a liquid state and generally come from plant sources. Saturated fats are solid and generally come from animal sources. Trans fats are a third major fat. These fats are often produced by companies trying to increase the shelf life of their products. Trans fats are unsaturated fats that are turned into saturated fats by hydrogenizing the unsaturated fat. Needless to say, trans fats are super bad and should be avoided.

Plant-based oils are a great vegan source of unsaturated fats. Butters like cocoa butter and coconut cream are also great sources of healthy vegan fats. There have been studies stating coconut oil is "overrated" as it only temporarily aids your body's nutritional levels. In fact, while coconut oil may claim to decrease LDL levels (your "bad" cholesterol levels) it actually eventually adds to your LDL levels in the long run. As a result, while many recipes lean towards the use of coconut oil, remember that any oil of your choice works just as well. These include sunflower oil, flax seed oil and olive oil, which give your body a well-balanced array of fats.

Omega 3-6-9

Fatty acids are vital for your body's functions, from your respiratory and circulatory systems to your brain and other vital organs. Ultimately, while the body does produce fatty acids such as the Omega-9 fatty acid on its, there are two essential fatty acids (EFAs) it cannot produce: Omega-3 and Omega-6.

The Omega-3 fatty acid is responsible for aiding in brain function as well as preventing cardiovascular disease. This fatty acid prevents asthma, certain cancers, arthritis, high cholesterol, blood pressure and so on. Many say that our dosage of Omega-3 can be satisfied by consuming fatty fish such as salmon however, it's a great misconception that vegans lack this vital nutrient due to not consuming fatty-flesh foods. While Omega-3 is most popularly taken from fish, it has a plethora of vegan sources as well, including green vegetables, chia seed oil, flaxseed oils, raw walnuts and hempseed oil to name a few!

The Omega-6 fatty acid is responsible for many of the benefits mentioned above when consumed with Omega-3. Omega-6 can be found in seeds, nuts, green veggies and oils, such as olive oil. The trick is to consume the right levels of these nutrients; you should be consuming double the amount of Omega-6 fatty acid as the Omega-3 or the benefits of these EFAs may actually be cancelled. The world has become victim to fast food and frozen pre-made dishes that have dangerously high amounts of Omega-6, but following a whole foods based diet can ensure your health as you get balanced amounts of each and every nutrient.

The Omega-9 fatty acid is a non-essential fatty acid which the body can produce. Although the body will only produce this fatty acid once there are appropriate levels of both Omega-3 and Omega-6, thus making it dependent on the consumption of the two fatty acids the body cannot produce. If you do not have appropriate amounts of Omega-3 and Omega-6, then you can get additional Omega-9 from your diet (since your body wouldn't be producing it in this case). Omega-9 can be found naturally in avocados, nuts, chia seed oil and olive oil.

Carbs

Carbohydrates are the human body's main energy source and are classed into two groups: simple and complex. Simple carbohydrates are low in nutrients and fiber and are easily broken down into glucose to generate energy. Complex carbohydrates consist of long chains of monosaccharides which take longer to be broken down. Unlike simple carbohydrates, they contain fiber (which keeps you satiated longer after a meal), minerals and vitamins. Complex carbohydrate plant sources include whole grains, lentils, legumes, beans, sweet potatoes and cruciferous vegetables.

The Glycemic Index (GI) is a scale used to rank carbohydrates according to the rise of glucose levels in the blood after consumption. High GI carbs release glucose into the blood very rapidly, commonly known as blood sugar spikes.

These blood sugar spikes caused by simple carbs should be avoided and can eventually be the cause of diabetes type 2. Complex carbs release glucose slowly because of a low GI (less than 55). Complex carbs are helpful in keeping a stable blood sugar level and should be a staple in your diet.

Micronutrient Intake

Micronutrients (vitamins and minerals) play important roles in most of the body's functions. Vitamins fall into two categories: water-soluble vitamins (C and B complex) and fat-soluble vitamins (A, D, E & K) – see chart below. Water-soluble vitamins are held in the body for up to three days and therefore need to be replaced regularly throughout the diet while fat-soluble vitamins can be stored in the liver for up to a year.

On a vegan diet, particular attention needs to be paid to vitamin D, calcium and vitamin B12. Vitamin B12, which plays a vital role in the procession of oxygen-carrying red blood cells, is predominantly found in animal products. Based on recommendations, an adult should consume 2.4mcg of vitamin B12 per day. On a vegan diet it would be wise to supplement and be vigilant about consuming foods such as B12-fortified cereals. Please talk to your nutritionist or dietician about the best way to supplement.

Good plant sources of calcium include leafy greens such as collards and kale, as well as plant-based milk alternatives like soy, almond, rice, or hemp milk. Vitamin D sources include Portobello and Shiitake mushrooms, as well as fortified milk alternatives. Though the best source of vitamin D is, of course, sunlight, if you live in a predominantly cloudy region of the world, it's a good idea to supplement.

Daily Needs of Micronutrients

Micronutrient	Recommended Dietary Allowance
Calcium	1200 mg
Phosphorus	700 mg
Magnesium	400 mg for men and 310 mg for women
Potassium	4700 mg
Sodium	1500 mg
Chloride	2300 mg

Iron	8 mg for men and 18 mg for women
Zinc	11 mg for men, 8 mg for women
Copper	900 μg
Iodine	150 μg
Manganese	2.3 mg for men, 1.8 mg for women
Vitamin A	900 μg for men, 700 μg for women
Vitamin D	15 μg
Vitamin E	15 mg
Vitamin K	120 μg for men, 90 μg for women
Vitamin C	90 mg for men, 75 mg for women
Thiamine (B1)	1.2 mg for men, 1.1 mg for women
Riboflavin (B2)	1.3 mg for men, 1.1 mg for women
Niacin (B3)	16 mg for men, 14 mg for women
Pantothenic acid (B5)	1.3 mg
Pyridoxine (B6)	1.3 mg
Biotin (B7)	30 μg
Folic acid (B9)	400 μg
Cobalamin/Vitamin B12	2.4 μg

Eating healthy and losing weight

Through preparing and storing meals, you will also be able to learn how to control your portion intake, since you will be using containers made up of compartments intended for the separation of meal components into the desired portions. When dividing portions, there are a number of aspects to consider, including calorie count and macronutrient proportions.

Taking in a lower number of calories will help you shed some weight.

The number of daily calories required in order to lose weight are shown in the percentage-based caloric deficit table below. These will not be empty calories as the vegan meals you prepare will be packed with nutrition to increase performance, brainpower and general health.

Be sure to note the nutritional information of each meal on the storage containers you use, as well as the weight of the portion. Once your containers are labeled, you can estimate the daily amount of calories and macros you will be taking in. To make it easy sticking to the caloric deficit required to achieve your goals, calculating your daily caloric needs will be explained in the subchapter "Counting calories".

Daily Caloric Needs	20% Caloric Deficit
1600 calories	320 calories below the maintenance level (1280 calories on a daily basis)
1800 calories	360 calories below the maintenance level (1440 calories on a daily basis)
2000 calories	400 calories below the maintenance level (1600 calories on a daily basis)
2500 calories	500 calories below the maintenance level (2000 calories on a daily basis)
3000 calories	600 calories below the maintenance level (2400 calories on a daily basis)
4000 calories	800 calories below the maintenance level (3200 calories on a daily basis)

Macros

Macronutrients or "macros" is the name given to three groups of energy-dense nutrients which make up the most basic components of our diets: carbohydrates, fats, and proteins. In addition to acting as fuel for bodily energy, they facilitate many of our bodies' functions and are broken down by our digestive system for use in bodily structures. Each macronutrient provides us with the following number of calories:

1 g protein = 4 calories

1 g carb = 4 calories

1 g fat = 9 calories

Simple physical activity to help weight loss

Some level of regular physical activity is a necessity for any successful weight loss program. Unfortunately, there is no way around it. You don't need to work out in a gym for two hours every day but you do need to have daily physical activity of at least 30-45 minutes. You simply cannot elevate your metabolism enough to lose weight without any exercise. There is no magic pill or potion that is going to make you achieve sustainable, healthy weight reduction without any exercise.

The healthiest time to exercise is two hours after a meal because your body has had time to digest your food and your blood can flow to your muscles instead of being diverted to your digestive tract to digest your food. The time that is most ideal for fat burning and quickly transforming your body is in the morning, before you have eaten any carbohydrates. This is because your body is coming out of a fasting state and it will have a lot of stored sugars for energy.

Your body will adapt if you engage in the same routine daily and lessen its beneficial effects. For instance, you can take a brisk walk, bicycle ride, use an elliptical machine, take a fitness class, do Pilates, yoga, or walk or run up and down an incline. The point is to try to vary your workout if possible, don't let your body adapt to the same daily regimen. Other great exercises are jumping rope, rowing, and circuit training in a gym.

Reasons Why You Should Exercise:
- Dramatically increases your weight loss
- Build and tone muscle
- Increase your metabolic rate
- Increase your immune system's ability to combat disease
- Slow down aging and prevent osteoporosis
- Improve your mental outlook by looking and feeling better

How does yoga benefit women?

Practicing yoga can provide a woman with both expected and unexpected benefits in the mind, body and spirit. Yoga offers you joy, reflection, solace and acceptance of your body.

Yoga can help you to find balance, both physically and emotionally. It can help you to accept yourself, too. It aids in your physical balance, but also brings balance to your life, giving you a clearer perspective.

The postures of yoga are helpful in relieving stress and in losing weight more easily. Yoga allows you to connect with your inner self. You can work into a pose and be just yourself, listening to your breathing and appreciating what your body can do.

All Women Can Benefit from Yoga You can embrace yoga regardless of your age; it will support you wherever you are in life. Your yoga will evolve and become more complete as you age, becoming wiser and more intuitive.

With the pressures of daily life today, you will find support from other women who feel the same way as you about finding themselves and learning what is important to them.

Standing poses like the Tree Pose and Warrior Pose will help you find physical and emotional strength. The Camel Pose will help you in finding compassion and openness. The Corpse Pose and Child's Pose will give you a sense of being grounded in yourself.

PMS strains your body. You can use yoga poses to counteract those effects. Likewise, poses in yoga can help you deal with the changes in your body that come with menopause. Standing poses help to prevent bone loss and increase circulation during menopause.

Connecting to your Body Before yoga, you may never have connected with your body. This could be due to limited physical activity or a lack of self-acceptance. Yoga gives you a chance to use your body and mind, and opens up a new world for you, if you have not previously been accepting of yourself.

Yoga helps you to appreciate your own outer and inner beauty, allowing you to breathe, move and live. Yoga can assist you in appreciating the miracle of your body, where you can overcome negative habits and learn to love yourself.

Weight Loss Benefits of Yoga

There's a lot of work involved in losing weight. You have to pay close attention to your diet and all the things you eat and don't eat. You have to make sure you're getting enough exercise and burning more calories than you're eating. It can be all-consuming. Yoga can help you stay balanced and focused on the positive aspects of what you're doing, rather than the hard work and the deprivation. There are a number of ways that yoga can benefit your weight loss plans. Regular yoga practice treats your mind and your body. It burns calories and fat, gives your heart a cardio workout and brings an element of peace and mindfulness to your weight loss journey.

Body
Not a lot of people realize what a productive calorie burner yoga can be. It's not going to have you jumping and sweating like running, basketball or cross training.

However, you do get a consistent calorie burn every time you dedicate 30 minutes or 60 minutes to yoga. Even a beginning yoga routine, with poses and positions found in Hatha yoga, allows you to burn around 300 calories in an hour. If you're going to pick up the pace a bit and do a more intense form of yoga such as Ashtanga or Vinyasa, you'll be able to burn even more. Movement of any kind provides the opportunity to burn calories.

The awareness of your body is another critical weight loss benefit when you're doing yoga. Each position and each pose requires you to focus on what your body is doing and how you are moving. You will be mindful of how the parts of your body work together and you'll be intimately in touch with each muscle and limb.

Flexibility is a huge benefit to doing yoga. All of the stretching you do will increase your balance and your ability to move. You'll notice your posture improves as well as the way you breathe and move. This might not seem like it would have an essential impact on losing weight, but it does. When you're able to move with more ease, your physical fitness level increases naturally. That keeps you moving and melting fat off your body. More flexibility means better fitness. You will notice that you look better in your clothes and you feel better when you are doing even simple things.

Mind
Yoga blends physical fitness with emotional and mental fitness. A large part of successful weight loss is positive thinking. When you incorporate a regular yoga practice into your weight loss strategy, you are training your mind to harness the power of intention and positivity. As you are stretching and holding poses, you can take the opportunity to visualize yourself as thinner, stronger and healthier. Existing in a state of expectation will help weight loss flow to you naturally. The mind is a powerful weapon in your weight loss battle and yoga will help you get in touch with that intention and put it to work for you.

Weight management is about managing stress as much as it's about cutting out the junk food and increasing the physical activity. When you get anxious or overwhelmed, your emotional imbalance can drive you towards bad habits. Yoga keeps you calm and trains you to lead yourself back to a state of peace when stress starts to invade your body and mind. That mindfulness will keep you balanced and positive.

Harnessing the Benefits
There are a number of practical ways to harness the weight loss benefits of yoga. When you're doing yoga, do it in a room without mirrors. A lot of yoga studios have mirrors, but try to avoid them. You want to remain positive and focused and if you're distracted by the sight of your thighs, you're disrupting your practice.

Talk to yourself in positive terms. This will make you feel better about yourself and will also keep the entire weight loss process positive and not negative. Practice what's called "self-talk." As you're involved in yoga, talk to yourself with supportive words and motivational phrases. Be consistent with your yoga as well. Go to classes regularly or set aside a specific amount of time every day to focus on yoga.

Creating a better body does not have to be a struggle or a negative process. You can achieve dramatic weight loss results by making small but meaningful changes to your life.

One of those changes is yoga. In addition to eating well and exercising in a way that works for you, incorporate yoga and take advantage of the various physical and mental benefits that come with it. You'll continue losing weight and you'll also have a more positive, more mindful and more balanced outlook on your life and the body you're creating.

Select suitable sports to change your physique

I challenge you to change your perspective about exercise. For most people, saying the word "exercise" gives us the same queasy stomach feeling as "IRS, taxes, or lawyer." Instead of instantly imagining barbells, fitness clubs, and expensive personal trainers, consider another option. Consider being physically active, not necessarily exercising.

When people decide they want to get healthier and lose some weight, they start by researching the newest and usually expensive workout programs, local fitness facilities, and they also look online for expensive exercise equipment. Again, in order to make progress or show commitment most people feel like they need to lay some serious cash down to start the process. This is completely wrong. In fact, it is literally working against your success and results. I'm not saying personal trainers, gym memberships or buying workout programs and equipment won't help at all or can't be effective.

What I'm saying is it is often unnecessary and expensive. After you've been active or working out for a month or two, you may feel ready to get more intense and focused on your activities or workouts. At that point, it makes complete sense to consider hiring someone to help or buying a program or product to move you forward with the habits you've already formed.

My perspective is to start simple and low cost and only then should you proceed with getting more complicated and expensive. Find an activity such as a daily walk, bike ride or a light weight program you can do at home for free. Do this DAILY for a month or two to get your body used to the activity. This will help your endurance, flexibility, and strength while preventing injury. Also, the activity doesn't have to be the same every day. Maybe one day you walk to the store and the next you ride your bike to a friend's house.

Stretching
Stretching is an awesome way to improve flexibility and prevent injury.

There are a million different stretching programs available for free online. Also, yoga stretches and poses are very helpful to improve flexibility and reduce injury. Search for a PDF version of one designed by a medical clinic or physical therapy office, print it, and hang it up where you will be finishing your walk, light weight program or bike ride. Only stretch AFTER you are active. Never stretch much before being active. Muscles, tendons, ligaments and joints are not as flexible when they are cold.

Walking

By far the most effective habit for weight loss and to improve your overall health is to go for a daily walk.

The benefits are significant and if you start walking daily, you will experience a transformation in your health and quality of life. How can this be? It's because a brisk, daily walk gives you a good chunk of time to get away, relax, and enjoy some time to yourself. These days, having some time to yourself during the day is hard to find. Remember, the goal of any activity recommendations in this book is not to add yet another activity to your life but to get more value and benefit from the activities you already do.

Instead of committing to some expensive or complicated exercise regimen, just start going for a simple walk once a day. Take a family member or friend and go explore your neighborhood or community. Maybe make a habit that you can't have dinner or sit down to watch television or use the computer until you've gone for your walk. Once you have done this for a month or so, this will become a habit and you'll look forward to it. At this point you will be able to decide what to do next. Do you go farther, faster, or maybe start lifting some weights? Do you decide to add some stairs or maybe riding a bike next time? It's really up to you but remember, you need to walk before you run! Be sure to get your heart rate pumping a bit, maybe even a slight sweat and you'll know you are working hard enough. If you aren't able to talk while you are being active, then you are working too hard and need to dial it back a bit.

Our lifestyles have changed over time reducing the amount of activity we are getting both at work and at play. How many neighborhoods do you drive through in your town and see kids everywhere on their bikes and outside playing? It's very rare and ultimately the research reveals this is becoming a serious issue in our society, as children are much less active and the rates of obesity and Type 2 diabetes in kids as young as ten years old are growing rapidly.

Running or Jogging

Before you start running, it is important that you make sure that running is the right option for you. There are certain factors that could put you at a higher risk for injury or other negative side effects: being over forty years of age, not accustomed to exercise, twenty pounds or more overweight, or a prior injury. If any of these factors apply, or if you have any concerns, consult your doctor before starting a running program.

Whether or not you consult with your doctor, you should still make sure to take it slowly when starting a running program. If you rush, you are likely to get discouraged, and possibly to injure yourself. Set a goal of being able to run continuously for thirty minutes – this will get you a great workout with a high level of calories burnt – but accept that it could take you quite a while to get there. Every person will go at his or her own pace. Set yourself reasonable goals; do not go too easy on yourself, but also do not expect too much.

In order to successfully implement running as part of your weight loss journey, you will need to schedule your workouts. Just like with taking the time to eat proper meals and snacks, if you do not take the time to get in a run then it is just not going to happen.

You need to consciously commit the time to exercising. Put each workout into your calendar, or find some other way to make sure that you remember when you are supposed to go. And follow that schedule, regardless of the many excuses that you will likely be able to come up with as to why you should not, or do not, need to go running that day.

Try to start by running four minutes then walking for one minute; experiment to see what works for you. Gradually build up the time in which you can run continuously until you are able to run for the entire twenty minutes.

Do not worry about how fast you are going; your speed will increase as you build up your stamina.

Pushups and Sit-ups
Start by doing a couple pushups and see you many you can do. Strive to do this several times daily and see how many you can do in a day! Try and do at least five of each exercise twice a day and soon it will be a habit which can make the difference in your upper body strength and core strength. If pushups are tough, start in a kneeling position instead of stretching out to balance on your toes, this is a bit easier and can help prevent injury as you are starting out.

You can find some fun push-up and sit-up programs free online which can help you stay consistent. There is also at least one free app for your phone and tablet which will remind you and keep count of your pushups each day. Before long you'll be able to drop and give me twenty without even a sweat!

Treadmill and Riding Your Bike
Having a treadmill or stationary bike in your home is incredibly helpful for getting your daily activity completed. Based on that experience, you'll be able to decide how much you want to do the next day. The goal is to increase the time you are riding every week so you see progress. I recommend buying an inexpensive dry erase white board calendar and putting it up on the wall next to the treadmill or stationary bike. Write down either the time, distance or both of these each day and you'll see these numbers increase over time! It's very rewarding.

Weight lifting
Lifting weights is an incredible way to improve strength, flexibility, and endurance.

Lifting weights can be completed with equipment at home or in the gym. Free weights or resistance bands seem to be the best and least expensive option. Using free weights and bands will also help build balance and coordination in your muscles to hold up a weight or perform reps correctly. Weight lifting machines can be used if you already have a gym membership however it's not necessary.

There are tons of resources online to help you with starting a basic weight lifting program. Again, I recommend finding a cheap set of dumbbells, barbells, or resistance bands on Craigslist or some other local used site. Don't buy new unless you absolutely have to. Simply go online and you can find awesome sites with tons of helpful information. Stay away from any website which charges you a fee to use it or is trying to sell you something.

Swimming

Lap swimming, water aerobics and aqua classes are probably the easiest on your body of any exercises. That doesn't mean they're easy, it just means they aren't as tough on your body. Movement in water is easier on your joints and back than land-based exercise. Lap swimming is a great way to get aerobic exercise without the jarring effects of the ground. Even though it does require access to a swimming pool, it doesn't require much else besides a swimsuit, goggles and a swim cap. Most fitness facilities with pools generally provide relatively inexpensive swim lessons and classes on how to swim if you need to learn or hone your skills. Water-based aerobics classes aren't just for grandmas anymore. Many wellness centers even offer sessions where yoga is performed on paddle boards. Don't rush out and pay for an expensive gym membership just to use the pool. If you already have a membership, that's great. But if not, keep your cash and just start with the other forms of activity for now.

Simple Sleep Truth

Sleep, sleep, sleep. There is nothing that will help you weight loss more than the right amount of sleep and rest. You cannot make any excuse for this. Some people get by on little sleep when they are younger and stay thin, if this is not you then you have a different type of body. You have to rearrange everything you do in order to sleep on a schedule and have a rhythm that your body can count on. You can step outside the schedule once a week, but otherwise your body looks for repetition to make it feel safe and rested. Everything you think you do when you do not get enough sleep can be done with enough sleep. It just becomes a matter of rearranging your schedule to fit everything in.

A great sleep pattern is to go to bed around 9 or 10 and get up at about 5 or 6 am. At first you might be a little resistant if you have not usually been sleeping on this schedule.

A really bad thing is to sleep strange times and different amounts on a regular basis. The right amount of sleep helps you have the proper emotional state of mind. Sleep is when the body repairs itself. Sleep keeps your natural system working the way it is supposed to for proper immune system function.

Four-week meal plan recipes

Here is your monthly plan, with all the recipes. Pay attention to the snacks that are offered here. They are intended primarily for those who do sport, and you must ensure a correct daily calorie intake.

If your life is sedentary or nearly so, then you have to calculate that the snack, for at least 5 days out of 7 in your week, can not be other than fruits and vegetables. You can choose those following the table that is proposed here. Snacks based on fruits and vegetables can also be eaten outside the home. Choose fruit that you can peel with ease, or raw vegetables that you can easily prepare, even the evening before, and store in the fridge in a container, ready to be put in the bag the next morning.

A tip is to hang this list in a visible place to decide which fruits/vegetables to eat in larger quantities and which in smaller quantities, or to calculate the calories you are taking in every day. The value refers to an amount of about 100 grams. Don't forget that fennel, cucumber and celery are your first ally for weight loss: the calories that are used to assimilate and digest them are higher than those introduced by eating them!

14 cal/cup	Cucumber, Celery
19 cal/cup	Radish
27 cal/cup	Fennel
28 cal/cup	Bell pepper
46 cal/cup	Watermelon
52 cal/cup	Cranberries, Carrot
53 cal/cup	Melon, Strawberries
57 cal/cup	Apple
60 cal/cup	Peach
64 cal/cup	Raspberries, Grapes
70 cal/cup	Currant
73 cal/cup	Apricot
74 cal/cup	Grapefruit
76 cal/cup	Plum
85 cal/cup	Orange, Pineapple
93 cal/cup	Pear
99 cal/cup	Mango
108 cal/cup	Kiwi, Tangerines, Fig
133 cal/cup	Banana
144 cal/cup	Pomegranate

DAY 1

Breakfast: Orange French toast

Preparation time: 5 minutes
Cooking time: 12 minutes
Servings: 4

Ingredients For French Toast
2-1/2 cups of almond milk, unsweetened
1 cup of almond flour
2 cups of applesauce
4 tablespoons of maple syrup, pure
½ teaspoon of cinnamon powder
Salt to taste
1 tablespoon of orange zest
12 whole-grain bread slices

Ingredients for Berry Compote
1 cup raspberries, fresh
1 cup applesauce
1 teaspoon of pure maple syrup

Directions
Preheat the oven to 400 degrees F.
Take a mixing bowl and mix almond milk, almond flour, maple syrup, cinnamon, salt, and applesauce. Mix the ingredients well. Transfer the mixture to any shallow pan and add orange zest to it. Mix all the ingredients well.
Heat a nonstick skillet, and start dipping each bread piece into a pan mixture.
Soak for a few seconds, then place it in the skillet and cook over medium for 2 minutes per side.
Place the cooked toast on serving plate and bake in the oven for 10 minutes to make it crisper.
Now, make a berry compote. Combine berries, applesauce, and maple syrup in a blender and pulse until smooth. Serve it with French toasts. Enjoy.

Nutritional Facts Per Serving
Calories: 240, Fat: 4 g, Carbs: 45 g, Protein: 4 g, Fiber:4 g

Lunch: Coconut Cauliflower Curry

Preparation time: 8 minutes
Cooking time: 20 minutes
Servings: 6-8

Ingredients
1 yellow onion
1 pound sweet potato, chopped
1 head cauliflower, chopped
2 tablespoons olive oil
1 teaspoon of salt (or to taste), divided 2 tablespoons curry powder
1 tablespoon Garam Masala
1 teaspoon cumin
¼ teaspoon cayenne
30 ounces of diced tomatoes
15 ounces can full-fat coconut milk
15 ounces chickpeas
4 cups spinach leaves
2 cups of brown rice, uncooked

Directions
The first step is to prepare the brown rice according to the package. Meanwhile, heat olive oil in a nonstick skillet and add onions to it.
Cook onions for 2 minutes, then add sweet potatoes and sauté for 3 minutes. Next, add salt and cauliflower, cook for 5 minutes.
Add curry powder and Garam Masala, cumin, cayenne, and tomatoes. Cook for 5 minutes and add coconut milk. Simmer the mixture for 5 minutes and then add drained chickpeas and 4 cups of spinach.
Stir it for 2 minutes and cook it until spinach is wilted. Once cooked, serve over cooked, steamed rice.

Nutritional Facts Per Serving
Calories: 200, Fat: 5 g, Carbs: 22 g, Protein: 5 g, Fiber:9 g

Dinner: Dinnertime Vegetable Soup

Preparation time: 10 minutes
Cooking time: 40 minutes
Servings: 4

Ingredients
6 cups organic vegetable broth
1 cup of water
1 onion, chopped
4 garlic cloves, chopped
1 beet peeled and chopped
2 cups Brussels sprouts, cut in half
2 cups carrot juice
1/3 cup green lentils, uncooked
1/4 cup red lentils, uncooked
1 cup kidney beans, organic
20 ounces of tomato sauce
1/3 teaspoon cinnamon
1/3 teaspoon Garam Masala
2 tablespoons of peanut butter
Sea salt and black pepper, to taste

Directions
Take a large cooking pot and add garlic, onions, and water in it. Then add vegetable broth, and cook until wilted. Add cinnamon powder and Garam Masala. Adjust salt by taste.
Now, add chopped vegetables and sauté for 10 minutes. Next, add red lentils, green lentils, carrot juice, beans, and tomato sauce. Stir in the butter.
Simmer it for 30 minutes by covering with the lid.
Once the soup is ready, and ingredients are tender, serve.

Nutritional Facts Per Serving
Calories: 340, Fat: 5 g, Carbs: 35 g, Protein: 5 g, Fiber: 12 g

Snack: Roasted Chickpeas

Preparation time: 5 minutes
Cooking time: 15 minutes
Servings: 3

Ingredients
16 ounces of chickpeas, drained and rinsed
2 teaspoons of olive oil
2 teaspoons of lemon juice, freshly squeezed
2 tablespoons of tamari sauce
Salt, pinch
¼ cup of agave nectar

Directions
Preheat the oven to 420 degrees F.
Layer the baking sheet with parchment paper.
In a bowl, add all the ingredients and toss well. And layer the chickpeas on a baking sheet.
Bake in oven until the chickpeas absorb the ingredients.
Serve at room temperature.

Nutritional Facts Per Serving
Calories: 190, Fat: 7 g, Carbs: 18 g, Protein: 12 g, Fiber:10 g

DAY 2

Breakfast: Chocolate Chip Coconut Pancakes
Preparation time: 10 minutes
Cooking time: 10 minutes
Servings: 4

Ingredients
2 tablespoons of flaxseed
1-1/2 cups of buckwheat flour
1/3 cup old-fashioned rolled oats
3 tablespoons unsweetened coconut flakes
½ tablespoon baking powder
Pinch of salt
1 cup unsweetened almond milk
1/3 cup unsweetened applesauce
1/3 cup pure maple syrup
1 teaspoon pure vanilla extract
⅓ cup chocolate chips, unsweetened

Directions
Pour water (about ½ cup) in a bowl and add flax seeds to it. Cook the flax seeds over medium heat. Once the mixture gets thick, strain the flax seeds mixture into a cup and set aside. Discard the seeds.
Take a mixing bowl and mix buckwheat, oats, coconut flakes, baking powder, and salt.
In a medium bowl, mix together applesauce, milk, maple syrup, vanilla, and reserved flaxseed water. Mix dry mixture to liquid mixture.
Now, stir in the chocolate chip. Now, heat a griddle over the medium heat and pour the batter of pancake on to the griddle. Cook for 5 minutes. Once, the bubble form on top cook from the other side.
Once done, repeat with the remaining mixture; then serve and enjoy.

Nutritional Facts Per Serving
Calories: 305, Fat: 4 g, Carbs: 45 g, Protein: 6 g, Fiber:8 g

Lunch: Healthy Green Soup

Preparation time: 10 minutes
Cooking time: 20 minutes
Servings: 4

Ingredients
½ cups broccoli
6 cups vegetable broth, unsalted
1 cup of water
½ cup cauliflower florets
1 cup Bok Choy
2 teaspoons lemon juice
2 teaspoons five-spice powder
6 ounces of Snow peas, trimmed
Salt and black pepper, to taste

Directions
Place all the ingredients in the instant pot and lock the lid.
Set timer to 20 minutes at high. Once the timer beeps, release the steam naturally. Now transfer the soup to the blender and pulse it for a few minutes.
Before serving, re-heat it. Serve and enjoy.

Nutritional Facts Per Serving
Calories: 180, Fat: 2 g, Carbs: 16 g, Protein: 4 g, Fiber:12 g

Dinner: Tacos with Salsa

Preparation time: 5 minutes
Cooking time: 5 minutes
Servings: 4

Ingredients
30 ounces of pinto beans, rinsed and drained
4 tablespoons of Dijon mustard
2 teaspoon of maple syrup
½ cup ketchup
1 teaspoon of garlic
¼ teaspoon chili powder
Salt, to taste
2 cups of pineapple chunks
1/3 cup minced red onion
1/4 cup finely chopped cilantro
½ small green cabbage, sliced
4 radishes, sliced
1 lime, sliced
12 Tortillas

Directions
Drain and rinse the beans. Take a skillet and put the beans, mustard, ketchup, maple syrup, garlic powder, chili powder, salt, and garlic powder in it. Heat it over low heat.
Mix pineapple, red onions, and cilantro in a bowl and add salt to it.
Now slice the cabbage and radish along with lime.
Now start making tortilla by placing it over gas flame over medium for few seconds. Next, place the beans, cabbage, radish in a tortilla, and end with a squeeze of lime.
Top it off with pineapple salsa. Serve and enjoy.

Nutritional Facts Per Serving
Calories: 320, Fat: 5 g, Carbs: 40 g, Protein: 5 g, Fiber:8 g

Snack: Gluten-Free Pistachios

Preparation time: 5 minutes
Cooking time: 20 minutes
Servings: 4

Ingredients
2 cups pistachios, shelled and salted
2 tablespoons of pure maple syrup
½ teaspoon of ginger, powdered

Directions
Preheat the oven to 300 degrees F. Take a bowl and mix ginger and pistachio in it.
Pour maple syrup on top. Stir well for fine coating.
Layer the pistachios on a baking dish lined with parchment paper.
Bake it in the oven for 20 minutes.
Once nuts are crisp, take out from the oven and let it sit for cooling. Serve and enjoy.

Nutritional Facts Per Serving
Calories: 340, Fat: 3 g, Carbs: 40 g, Protein: 3 g, Fiber:4 g

DAY 3

Breakfast: Eggless Scrambles

Preparation time: 5 minutes
Cooking time: 5 minutes
Servings: 2

Ingredients
1 green onion, chopped
1-1/2 cup firm raw tofu, drained
1 small red tomatoes, chopped
½ teaspoon of turmeric
½ teaspoon of cumin
2 teaspoons of lemon juice
4 slices of Rye Bread, toasted
2 tablespoons of olive oil
½ teaspoon of sesame seeds
Salt and black pepper, to taste

Directions
Pour oil to a nonstick skillet. Now, add green onions to the pan.
Once, sizzling add tomatoes, lemon juice, cumin, sesame seeds, and turmeric.
Now add tofu and make a scramble in pan. Adjust seasoning by adding salt and black pepper.
Avoid overcooking and making it a mush. Now toast the bread and place a generous amount of scramble over bread slices. Serve and enjoy hot.

Nutritional Facts Per Serving
Calories: 190, Fat: 7 g, Carbs: 10 g, Protein: 12 g, Fiber: 4 g

Lunch: Simple Veggies Stew

Preparation time: 15 minutes
Cooking time: 20 minutes
Servings: 4

Ingredients
2 green zucchinis, chopped
½ tablespoon garlic powder
2 cups of water
½ cup turnip, peeled and chopped
2 cups of coconut milk
Salt, to taste
Black pepper, to taste
½ cup Swiss chard, chopped
½ cup spinach stems removed
½ cup Brussels sprout

Directions
Pour water in a cooking pan and let it boil over medium heat.
Now add zucchini, turnip, Swiss chard, spinach, and Brussels sprouts in the water and cook for 15 minutes covered. Now, add garlic powder, salt, and black pepper.
Simmer for 5 minutes and add coconuts milk.
Let it cook it for 12 more minutes, covered.
Once done, serve the stew. Enjoy.

Nutritional Facts Per Serving
Calories: 290, Fat: 7 g, Carbs: 20 g, Protein: 10 g, Fiber:12 g

Dinner: Green Gram Split Lentil Recipe

Preparation time: 45 minutes
Cooking time: 30 minutes
Servings: 2

Ingredients
1 cup of green gram split lentils, pre-soaked (without skin)
4 cups of water
2 garlic cloves, paste
½ teaspoon of ginger, paste
Salt, to taste
1 teaspoon organic coriander Powder
1/4 teaspoon organic turmeric Powder
4 teaspoons of olive oil
2 small red onions, chopped
1 teaspoon organic cumin
¼ teaspoon of red chili powder
2 green chilies, chopped

Directions
Soak the lentil for 40 minutes, before starting the cooking. Drain the lentils and set aside.
In a large cooking pot, add water, lentil, salt, onions, lentils, coriander powder, turmeric powder, chili powder, and cumin powder.
Bring it to boil and cook for 30 minutes covered.
Next, take a medium skillet and pour olive oil. Add garlic and ginger paste to it. Cook until lightly brown. Pour this mixture over the lentils. Mix the lentils, and then serve with green chili garnish if liked.

Nutritional Facts Per Serving
Calories: 210, Fat: 6 g, Carbs: 20 g, Protein: 12 g, Fiber:10 g

Snack: Cauliflower Poppers with Sauce

Preparation time: 10 minutes+24 Hours
Servings: 6

Ingredients
2 heads of cauliflower, florets
1 cup dates, pitted
½ cup of filtered water
½ cup sun-dried tomatoes
2 tablespoons nutritional yeast
4 tablespoons raw tahini
2 tablespoons apple cider vinegar
1 teaspoon cayenne pepper
1 teaspoon garlic powder
1 teaspoon onion powder
1 teaspoon turmeric

Directions
First, chop the cauliflower into bite-size pieces.
Next, take a high-speed blender and add all the other ingredients in it. Blend until reaching a thick consistency. Pour the sauce over cauliflower.
Toss the florets well for fine coating. Place the florets onto your dehydrator trays.
Dehydrate at 115 F for 12 - 24 hours.
Once desired crunchiness is reached serve and enjoy.

Nutritional Facts Per Serving
Calories: 180, Fat: 5 g, Carbs: 20 g, Protein: 5 g, Fiber:10 g

DAY 4

Breakfast: Breakfast Blueberries Pancakes
Preparation time: 10 minutes
Cooking time: 10 minutes
Servings: 3

Ingredients
2 cups spelt flour
1 scoop stevia
2 ripe bananas, mashed
1-1/4 cup cashew milk, unsweetened
½ cup blueberries, fresh and chopped
½ cup strawberries, fresh and chopped
1 cup almond flour
Oil spray for greasing

Directions
Mix spelt flour and almond flour in a large bowl. Pour milk in the flour and mix well. Add 2 bananas and combine ingredients. Stir the ingredients to make a runny consistency. Make sure no lumps remain. In the end, add stevia and chopped berries. If the consistency is too watery, then add a bit of more almond flour.
Grease a skillet or griddle with oil spray. Pour the spoon full of the mixture to the griddle. Once the bubbles form on the top, flip to cook on the other side. Serve and enjoy.

Nutritional Facts Per Serving
Calories: 280, Fat: 7 g, Carbs: 35 g, Protein: 5 g, Fiber:4 g

Lunch: Garlic Pasta

Preparation time: 10 minutes
Cooking time: 20 minutes
Servings: 3

Ingredients
2 cups of tomatoes, cut in half
12 ounces of whole wheat pasta, penne
2 tablespoons of olive oil
4 shallots, chopped
6 cloves of garlic
Salt and black pepper, to taste
6 tablespoons of almond flour
6 tablespoons of almond milk
3 cups of vegetable stock, unsweetened

Directions
Preheat the oven at 420 degrees F.
Toss the tomatoes in sea salt, black pepper, and 1 tablespoon of olive oil. Place the tomatoes on to the baking sheet lined with parchment paper. Bake it in the oven for 20 minutes.
Meanwhile, prepare pasta by bringing water to boil in a large pot. Cook pasta, according to package instruction.
Meanwhile, in a medium skillet, add remaining olive oil, garlic, almond flour, and shallots.
Add salt and black pepper. Cook it for 2 minutes. Add in almond milk a little at a time so no lumps remain. Then, add in the stock. Simmer and cook for 10 minutes.
Once the sauce is done, add the drained pasta to the sauce. Add roasted tomatoes on top.
Garnish it with the fresh basil. Serve and enjoy.

Nutritional Facts Per Serving
Calories: 420, Fat: 7 g, Carbs: 50 g, Protein: 5 g, Fiber: 6 g

Dinner: Roasted Cauliflower Soup

Preparation time: 10 minutes
Cooking time: 45 minutes
Servings: 6-8

Ingredients
4 pounds of cauliflower florets, chopped
1-1/2 cups leeks, chopped
1 cup olive oil
Salt and black pepper, to taste
½ cup parsley
1 cup chives, chopped
10 cups of vegetable broth, unsalted and unsweetened
5 teaspoons of white wine vinegar

Directions
Preheat the oven to 375 degrees F.
Grease a baking sheet with oil.
In a bowl, place leeks and cauliflower, and toss it with salt, black pepper, and 1 tablespoon of olive oil. Layer the vegetables in a baking sheet and bake for 30 minutes.
Meanwhile, blend the chives, parsley, salt, and black pepper to the paste.
Mix and add the remaining olive oil to the blender. Take out the roasted vegetables from the oven and add to the pot. Pour broth into the pot and bring the mixture to a boil. Simmer it for 15 minutes. Add in the white wine vinegar and cook for 5 minutes.
Then puree the mixture using a blender in batches. In the end, stir in the herb sauce or swirl it on top. Enjoy the soup hot.

Nutritional Facts Per Serving
Calories: 350, Fat: 7 g, Carbs: 20 g, Protein: 11 g, Fiber:6 g

Snack: Banana-Oat Protein Balls

Preparation time: 10 minutes
Servings: 4

Ingredients
1-1/2 cup rolled oats
1 scoop of protein powder
2 large bananas, ripe

Directions
Place oats, protein powder, and banana in a food processor.
Pulse it until smooth.
Roll into 12 balls.
Place in a reusable container or serve immediately.

Nutritional Facts Per Serving
Calories: 180, Fat: 1 g, Carbs: 20 g, Protein: 12 g, Fiber:9 g

DAY 5

Breakfast: Panini Recipe

Preparation time: 10 minutes
Servings: 2

Ingredients
½ cup of raisins
½ cup of hot water
½ tablespoon cinnamon
4 teaspoons cacao powder
1/3 cup of natural peanut butter
2 ripe bananas
4 slices of whole-grain bread

Directions
Combine raisins, hot water, cacao powder, and cinnamon in a bowl.
Take whole grain bread, and put butter on it.
Slice the bananas, and layer on bread. Blend raisin mixture in a blender and spread over bread. Serve.

Nutritional Facts Per Serving
Calories: 310, Fat: 2 g, Carbs: 25 g, Protein: 3 g, Fiber:5 g

Lunch: Quinoa Lime Burrito Bowl

Preparation time: 10 minutes
Cooking time: 45 minutes
Servings: 2

Ingredients:
2 cups quinoa
4 cups of water
1 teaspoon of chili powder
Salt, to taste
2 potatoes, cubed
2 cups black beans
3 cloves garlic, minced
1 small onion, diced
½ bell pepper, diced
1 cup cherry tomatoes
½ cup of cabbage
2 cups of baby spinach
2 avocados, sliced
2 limes, juiced
½ cup olive oil

Directions
Boil water in a cooking pot and cook quinoa in it for 15 minutes. Once, the quinoa gets fluffy and cooked add chili powder, and lime juice to it. Mix well, and let it sit for a while for further use.
Peel the potatoes, and toss in olive oil.
Season it with salt and roast in the oven for 20 minutes. Meanwhile, mix beans with garlic and heat in oven for 10 minutes.
In a mixing bowl, mix lime juice, salt, and olive oil. Now, divide the beans, quinoa, and potatoes among two bowls, and top with bell pepper, onions, cabbage, baby spinach, and tomatoes.
Garnish it with the avocado slices; adjust the seasoning and serve.

Nutritional Facts Per Serving:
Calories: 350, Fat: 10 g, Carbs: 35 g, Protein: 5 g, Fiber:9 g

Dinner: Rosemary Balsamic Roasted Vegetable

Preparation time: 8 minutes
Cooking time: 35 minutes
Servings: 2

Ingredients
1 pound of Brussels sprouts
½ medium cauliflower, florets
2 carrots, chopped
2 turnips, chopped and peeled
2 beets, peeled and chopped
2 sweet potatoes, peeled and chopped
3 tablespoons of balsamic vinegar
4 teaspoons of olive oil
2 teaspoons of honey
2 teaspoons of chopped rosemary
4 garlic cloves
1 teaspoon of onion powder
Salt and black pepper, to taste

Directions
Preheat the oven to 400 degrees F. Line the baking sheet with parchment paper. Spray oil on parchment paper.
Take a bowl and combine all the vegetables along with olive oil, balsamic vinegar, honey, rosemary, garlic cloves, onion powder, salt, and black pepper. Toss all the ingredients well.
Place the vegetable on parchment paper. Bake in the oven for 35 minutes. Once vegetables get tender, take out from the oven and serve.

Nutritional Facts Per Serving
Calories: 190, Fat: 4 g, Carbs: 18 g, Protein: 4 g, Fiber:16 g

Snack: Dark Chocolate Figs

Preparation time: 5 minutes
Cooking time: 1 minute
Servings: 4

Ingredients
1 cup chocolate, dark chocolate 100% cacao
16 fresh figs
1 cup raw walnuts, chopped

Directions
Put the chocolate in a microwave-safe bowl and melt in the microwave for a few seconds. Dip the figs into melted chocolate. Now place figs on parchment paper and sprinkle walnuts on top. Refrigerate for 20 minutes, once solid serve.

Nutritional Facts Per Serving:
Calories: 290, Fat: 7 g, Carbs: 38 g, Protein: 4 g, Fiber:4 g

DAY 6

Breakfast: Mushroom, Olives and Chickpea Omelette

Preparation time: 10 minutes
Cooking time: 10 minutes
Servings: 2

Ingredients
½ cup of chickpea flour
1 teaspoon of chopped onions
1 teaspoon of garlic minced
Salt and black pepper, to taste
1/3 cup nutritional yeast
1 teaspoon of baking soda
5 ounces sautéed mushrooms
2 ounces black olives, chopped
1 cup salsa

Directions
In a large mixing bowl add chickpea flour, onions, garlic, salt, black pepper, nutritional yeast, baking soda. Add about 1 cup of water to make a smooth paste.
Heat olive oil in a frying pan and pour the batter into the pan.
Sprinkle mushrooms and black olives over the batter. Once cooked from the bottom flip to cook on the other side.
Serve it with the topping of salsa. Enjoy hot.

Nutritional Facts Per Serving:
Calories: 250, Fat: 5 g, Carbs: 20 g, Protein: 8 g, Fiber:6 g

Lunch Tomato Soup

Preparation time: 10 minutes
Cooking time: 20 minutes
Servings: 2

Ingredients
6 cups tomatoes, chopped and peeled
1 teaspoon of olive oil
1 onion, peeled
4 cups vegetable broth
Salt and black pepper to taste
1 tablespoon maple syrup
2 teaspoons lemon juice
1/2 cup cream
½ cup of water

Directions
Boil the tomatoes in boiling water for 10 minutes. Peel the tomatoes and transfer to the blender. Blend to make smooth.
Take a skillet and add olive oil and onions. Cook for 3 minutes.
Pour the vegetable broth and add tomato puree and season it with salt and black pepper.
Simmer for a few minutes, and add maple syrup and lemon juice. Add a bit of water.
Cook for 5 more minutes. Then add half of the cream and cook 5 minutes.
Serve topped with the remaining cream.

Nutritional Facts Per Serving:
Calories: 220, Fat: 7 g, Carbs: 22 g, Protein: 8 g, Fiber:12 g

Dinner: Instant Pot Acorn Squash with Cranberries

Preparation time: 10 minutes
Cooking time: 10 minutes
Servings: 4

Ingredients
4 acorn squashes, trimmed and seedless
6 tablespoons of olive oil
2 shallots, chopped
12 ounces of mushrooms, chopped
4 garlic cloves, minced
1 cup cranberries

Directions
Pour the water in the instant pot, and adjust the trivet or steamer basket on top. Place the squash on top of the steamer basket. Lock the lid of the instant pot. Set a timer to 5 minutes at high pressure.
Once the timer beeps, release the steam naturally.
Take a medium pan and heat oil then add shallots, mushrooms, and garlic. Season it with salt and black pepper. Cook for a few minutes, then add cranberries and let it cook for 4 more minutes.
Open the instant pot, and pour the sauce ingredients on top. Serve.

Nutritional Facts Per Serving:
Calories: 310, Fat: 7 g, Carbs: 28 g, Protein: 8 g, Fiber: 12 g

Snack: Herb-Crusted Asparagus Spears

Preparation time: 10 minutes
Cooking time: 20 minutes
Servings: 2

Ingredients
10 asparagus, washed
2 teaspoons of flax seeds
1 teaspoon of hemp seeds
1 teaspoon of ginger paste
¼ teaspoon of garlic paste
Salt and black pepper to taste
¼ cup whole wheat bread crumbs
1 teaspoon of lime juice

Directions
Preheat your oven to 350°F.
Remove the white bottom from the end of the asparagus by snapping it off.
Combine all the remaining ingredients in a bowl and toss the asparagus with the mixture. Arrange asparagus on a baking sheet lined with parchment paper.
Bake it in ovens or 20 minutes. Once crispy, remove from oven.
Then serve and enjoy.

Nutritional Facts Per Serving:
Calories:150, Fat: 7 g, Carbs: 20 g, Protein: 6 g, Fiber:9 g

DAY 7

Breakfast: Whole-Wheat Berry Muffins
Preparation time: 10 minutes
Cooking time: 22 minutes
Servings: 4

Ingredients
½ cup almond milk
1-1/2 tablespoon ground flaxseeds
1 teaspoon apple cider vinegar
2-1/2 cups whole-wheat pastry flour
2 teaspoons baking powder
¼ teaspoon baking soda
1/4 teaspoon salt
1/3 cup applesauce, unsweetened
1/3 cup pure maple syrup
1-1/3 teaspoons pure vanilla extract
1-1/3 cup blueberries

Directions
Preheat the oven to 375 degrees F. Line a muffin tin with silicon liners. Take a measuring cup and mix almond milk, vinegar, and flaxseeds. Mix it vigorously for a few seconds.
Now, in a separate medium bowl, mix baking soda, baking powder, salt, and flour. Pour the milk mixture into the flour mixture. Next, add applesauce, vanilla, and maple syrup. Next, fold in the blueberries.
Fill the muffin cup with batter and bake it in the oven for 22 minutes. Once muffins are baked, let it get cooled completely for 10 minutes.
Remove from the tray and serve. Enjoy.

Nutritional Facts Per Serving:
Calories: 410, Fat: 3 g, Carbs: 40 g, Protein: 3 g, Fiber: 5 g

Lunch: Chickpea Cauliflower Quiche

Preparation time: 10 minutes
Cooking time: 30 minutes
Servings: 4

Ingredients
2 cups chickpea flour
2 tablespoons of flax meal
Salt and black pepper, to taste
1 teaspoon Italian seasoning or Herbs de Provence
½ teaspoon of baking powder
1 small head of cauliflower
1 cup of water
1 zucchini, sliced
1 red onion, sliced thinly
1 cup of fresh rosemary, chopped

Directions
Combine all the dry ingredients in a small bowl.
Now chop onions and zucchinis and process cauliflower in a blender. Add these vegetables to the bowl and mix in water. Stir in remaining ingredients. Mix well to a thick consistency.
Now, take an 8-inch silicon cake tin. Now spoon the mixture into the tin.
Bake in oven for 30 minutes, at 350 degrees F.
Once golden on the top, serve and enjoy.

Nutritional Facts Per Serving:
Calories: 320, Fat: 2 g, Carbs: 45 g, Protein: 3 g, Fiber: 8 g

Dinner: Indian Peanut Noodles

Preparation time: 10 minutes
Cooking time: 15 minutes
Servings: 4

Ingredients
2 cups of raw peanuts
1 teaspoon cumin powder
1 teaspoon red chili powder
10 ounces soba noodles
4 tablespoons vegetable oil
1 cup broccoli florets, chopped into 1-inch pieces
1 cup zucchinis, chopped
1 to 2 tablespoons light soy sauce, to taste
Salt, to taste

Directions
Roast the peanuts for 6 minutes in the microwave and then let it cool.
Now, to prepare the sauce, blend all the chutney ingredients in a blender. Cook the noodles according to package instruction. In a skillet heat oil and broccoli, and sauté for 5 minutes.
Then add other vegetables one by one. Do not overcook and make vegetables mushy.
Now add the chutney and mix well. Then add salt and soy sauce. Now add noodles and mix well. Serve it once done.

Nutritional Facts Per Serving:
Calories: 480, Fat: 5 g, Carbs: 50 g, Protein: 6 g, Fiber:10 g

Snack: Peanut Butter and Chocolate Bars

Preparation time: 10 minutes + 4 hours
Cooking time: 4 minutes
Servings: 6

Ingredients
½ cup of coconut oil
2 cups cocoa powder, unsweetened
1 cup of peanut butter, no added sugar
¼ cup stevia
Salt, pinch

Directions
Pour oil in the skillet and let it melt on low flame. Add butter and let it melt. Cook it for 30 seconds. Then add all the remaining ingredients and let it get combined well.
Cook utile all the ingredients are well combined and melted. Pour the mixture into the baking sheet lined with parchment paper.
Freeze it for 40 minutes. Once solid, serve it by cutting into bar shapes.

Nutritional Facts Per Serving:
Calories: 310, Fat: 15 g, Carbs: 20 g, Protein: 10 g, Fiber:3 g

DAY 8

Breakfast: Mason Jar Overnight Oats

Preparation time: 10 minutes
Servings: 2

Ingredients
½ cup gluten-free oats
1-1/4 cup almond milk
1 teaspoon of chia seeds
2 tablespoons maple syrup
½ teaspoon cinnamon
Dash of vanilla bean powder or extract
1 cup strawberries, chopped

Directions
Place oats, chia seeds, cinnamon, maple syrup, vanilla powder, and strawberries in a mason jar. Mix and seal the jar.
Refrigerate overnight. Next morning open the jar and mix the ingredients. Serve and enjoy.

Nutritional Facts Per Serving:
Calories: 220, Fat: 7 g, Carbs: 24 g, Protein: 4 g, Fiber: 6 g

Lunch: Cold Raw Peanut Soup

Preparation time: 10 minutes
Servings: 2

Ingredients
½ cup of raw peanuts
4 cups of water
1 cup broccoli, fresh or frozen
½ cup spinach, fresh or frozen
½ cup of leeks, sliced
½ garlic clove, chopped
½ teaspoon ginger, grated
1 tablespoon of lemon juice
Salt and black pepper, to taste

Directions
Dump all the ingredients in a high-speed blender and pulse until smooth.
Once a smooth consistency is obtained serve it cold. It is a great-tasting and versatile soup to enjoy.

Nutritional Facts Per Serving:
Calories: 130, Fat: 2 g, Carbs: 18 g, Protein: 4 g, Fiber:16 g

Dinner: Zucchini with Stuffing

Preparation time: 10 minutes
Cooking time: 27 minutes
Servings: 3

Ingredients
1-1/2 cup quinoa, rinsed
6 medium zucchini
1 cup cannellini beans, drained
2 large onions, chopped
½ cup black olives
½ cup almonds, chopped
4 cloves of garlic, chopped
2 tablespoons olive oil
1 cup of water
1 cup cream

Directions
Take an air fryer and preheat it at 375 degrees F for 5 minutes.
In a skillet, heat the oil and sauté onions and garlic. Cook onions for 2 minutes. Add quinoa and water. Let it cook for 5 minutes. Afterwards add cannellini beans, black olives, and almonds. Cook for 10 minutes.
Wash and cut the zucchini lengthwise and takeout the seeds. Fill the cavity of zucchinis with skillet mixture. Place it in air fryer and cook for 15 minutes. Afterward take out zucchini and top it with cream. Serve and enjoy.

Nutritional Facts Per Serving:
Calories: 280, Fat: 5 g, Carbs: 29 g, Protein: 6 g, Fiber:12 g

Snack: Carrot Cake Oatmeal

Preparation time: 5 minutes
Cooking time: 20 minutes
Servings: 4

Ingredients
2 cups almond milk
1 cup oats, whole grain
½ cup of water
1 cup shredded carrot
1/3 cup raisins
¼ teaspoon vanilla extract
¼ teaspoon of cinnamon
¼ teaspoon of allspice
Salt, dash

Topping Ingredients
4 tablespoons of maple syrup
1/3 cup chopped walnuts
4 tablespoons of coconut, shredded

Directions
In a medium cooking pot, pour the milk in and add oats along with water. Then cook for 10 minutes. Once started to simmer, add carrots, vanilla extract, cinnamon, raisins, allspice, and salt. Simmer for 10 more minutes.
Pour this mixture to the bowl and drizzle maple syrup on top. Add walnuts and coconut on top. Serve and enjoy.

Nutritional Facts Per Serving:
Calories: 310, Fat: 5 g, Carbs: 25 g, Protein: 4 g, Fiber:9 g

DAY 9

Breakfast: Oats Pancakes

Preparation time: 10 minutes
Cooking time: 10 minutes
Servings: 3

Ingredients
4 ripe bananas, peeled
2 1/2 cups rolled oats
1 1/2 cup almond milk
1 teaspoon of olive oil

Directions
Take a blender and add bananas, oats, and almond milk. Once the batter is a smooth consistency, pour into a bowl.
Take a skillet, and heat oil in it over medium flame. Now pour ½ cup of batter to the skillet and cook the pancakes. Once bubbles form on the top, flip to cook on the other side.
Once all batter is used, and pancakes are ready, serve. Enjoy

Nutritional Facts Per Serving:
Calories: 240, Fat: 4 g, Carbs: 30 g, Protein: 4 g, Fiber:6 g

Lunch: Avocado Toast

Preparation time: 10 minutes
Cooking time: 4 minutes
Servings: 2

Ingredients

4 slices of bread
2 avocados, slices
Juice of 1 lemon
4 tablespoons pumpkin seeds
¼ teaspoon of red pepper flakes
1/3 teaspoon of smoked paprika
¼ teaspoon of sesame seeds
Salt and black pepper, to taste

Directions

First step is to toast the bread. Now layer the avocado slices on the toast. Squeeze lemon juice on top.
End with the sprinkle of pumpkin seeds, sesame seeds, pepper flakes, salt and black pepper. Serve and enjoy.

Nutritional Facts Per Serving:

Calories: 310, Fat: 12 g, Carbs: 28 g, Protein: 4 g, Fiber:6 g

Dinner: Tofu and Peanut Satay

Preparation time: 10 minutes
Cooking time: 25 minutes
Servings: 2

Ingredients
1 block of firm tofu, cubed
1 cucumber, ribbon

Ingredients for Marinade
1 tablespoon of peanut butter
4 tablespoons of tamari sauce
1 tablespoons of sesame oil
4 tablespoons of maple syrup
2 garlic cloves

Ingredients for Satay Sauce
1/3 cup coconut milk
4 tablespoons of peanut butter
2 tablespoons of peanut butter
2 teaspoons of lime juice
2 teaspoons tamari sauce
4 teaspoons of maple syrup
2 small garlic clove, minced
2 teaspoons of ginger, minced
Salt and black pepper, to taste

Directions
First, make a marinade in a bowl by mixing all the marinade ingredients.
Now, let the tofu sit in the marinade for 15 minutes. Wash and peel the cucumber in thin ribbons.
Now, stir in the Satay ingredients together. Thread the marinated tofu onto skewers.
Place the skewers on the grill and grill on medium flame. Lightly oil it with oil spray. Grill the tofu until lightly browned.
Now threat the cucumber on a skewer by folding it back forth to it easy thread to the skewer.
Top it with Satay drizzle and serve.

Nutritional Facts Per Serving:
Calories: 360, Fat: 10 g, Carbs: 30 g, Protein: 14 g, Fiber:6 g

Snack: No Bake Oatmeal Bars

Preparation time: 10 minutes + 2 hours
Servings: 3

Ingredients
1 cup dates, soft and pitted
1/2 cup almonds
1/3 cup peanut butter, organic and all natural
2 tablespoons of maple syrup
3/4 cup oats
1/3 cup hemp seeds

Directions
Take a food processor and place dates and almonds. Blend to mix well. Then add oats, peanut butter, hemp seeds, maple syrup and pulse for a few minutes. Line a loaf pan with a parchment paper and press the prepared dough into the pan. Freeze until solid and then cut in to equal squares. Serve and enjoy.

Nutritional Facts Per Serving:
Calories: 310, Fat: 12 g, Carbs: 28 g, Protein: 9 g, Fiber:10 g

DAY 10

Breakfast: Triple Berry Porridge

Preparation time: 5 minutes
Cooking time: 10 minutes
Servings: 2

Ingredients
½ cup Steel Cut Oats
1/4 cup Quinoa
1-1/2 cups water
1 cup organic blueberries, frozen
2 tablespoons of Maple syrup, optional
1 teaspoon of hemp seeds, optional

Directions
Take an instant pot and combine oats, quinoa, and water. Lock the lid and set the timer to 10 minutes at high. Once timer beeps, release the steam naturally. Sir the mixture and transfer to a serving bowl.
Mix blueberries, maple syrup, and hemp seeds. Mix well and then serve.

Nutritional Facts Per Serving:
Calories: 290, Fat: 2 g, Carbs: 30 g, Protein: 8 g, Fiber:12 g

Lunch: Tofu Tikka Masala in Instant Pot

Preparation time: 10 minutes
Cooking time: 25 minutes
Servings: 4

Tofu Tikka Masala Ingredients
20 tablespoons thick coconut milk
1 teaspoon coriander powder
½ teaspoon Garam Masala
½ teaspoon red chili powder
½ teaspoon smoked paprika
Salt, to taste
400 grams extra-firm tofu

Curry Ingredients
4 tablespoons olive oil
3 red onion, chopped
3 garlic cloves, finely chopped
2-inches ginger, chopped
8 large tomatoes, pureed
1 teaspoon curry powder
½ teaspoon cumin powder
Salt, to taste
¼ teaspoon red chili powder
2 teaspoons honey
1 cup of coconut milk
1/2 cup water

Directions
Combine all the tofu Tikka Masala ingredients in a large bowl. Mix well and set it aside.
Now make curry. In a skillet heat oil and make curry by adding onions, ginger, garlic and tomatoes; cook it for about 5 minutes.
Then add remaining ingredients from the curry ingredients. Simmer it for 10 minutes.
Now, add tofu mixture from the bowl into the skillet. Close the lid and cook for 20 minutes. Once done, serve.

Nutritional Facts Per Serving:
Calories: 420, Fat: 6 g, Carbs: 30 g, Protein: 18 g, Fiber:12 g

Dinner: Simple Spinach Soup

Preparation time: 10 minutes
Cooking time: 14 minutes
Servings: 6

Ingredients
10 cups vegetable broth
1 cup tomatoes, un-drained
1 cup spinach, thawed and drained
Salt and black pepper, to taste
½ cup carrot
4 cloves garlic, minced
1 onion, peeled and chopped
⅓ cup celery
½ teaspoon chili powder
¼ teaspoon curry powder
2 cups of coconut milk

Directions
Combine all ingredients in an Instant Pot. Set timer for 12 minutes at high pressure.
After 12 minutes, let the pressure release naturally. Turn on the sauté mode and add milk, cook for 2 minutes. Serve in soup bowls.

Nutritional Facts Per Serving:
Calories: 270, Fat: 2 g, Carbs: 20 g, Protein: 6 g, Fiber:20 g

Snack: Strawberries Popsicles

Preparation time: 10 minutes
Servings: 2

Ingredients
½ cups coconut milk
4 cups strawberries
2 scoops of stevia
1/3 cup water

Directions
Blend all the listed ingredients in a blender and pulse it into a smooth paste.
Refrigerate for a few hours or overnight.
Once, solid enjoy as a sweet snack time treat.

Nutritional Facts Per Serving:
Calories: 130, Fat: 1 g, Carbs: 20 g, Protein: 2 g, Fiber:6 g

DAY 11

Breakfast: Keto Cinnamon Coffee

Preparation time: 5 minutes
Servings: 2

Ingredients
4 teaspoons of ground coffee
1 teaspoon of cinnamon
2 cups of water, hot

Directions
Take coffee brewer, and mix cinnamon powder and ground coffee.
Pour in piping hot water into the brewer. Let it brew. Then press it and pour it into the cup. Serve.

Nutritional Facts Per Serving:
Calories: 30, Fat: 0 g, Carbs: 6 g, Protein: 0 g, Fiber:3 g

Lunch: Baked Veggies with Sauce

Preparation time: 10 minutes
Cooking time: 30 minutes
Servings: 2

Main Ingredients
2 cups raw broccoli, chopped
¼ cup cauliflower florets
¼ cup cabbage
¼ cup kale
¼ small tomatoes, chopped

Sauce Ingredients
2 ounces chia seeds
10 tablespoons almonds
1 lime, juiced
1 tablespoons garlic
Salt and black pepper
4 tablespoons of olive oil

Directions
Pulse all the sauce ingredients in the blender to prepare a paste.
In a bowl, combine all the ingredients listed below the main ingredients.
Drizzle the blended sauce over the top.
Bake it on the oven for 375 degrees for about 30 minutes.
Once baked, take out from the oven and enjoy.

Nutritional Facts Per Serving:
Calories: 300, Fat: 6 g, Carbs: 22 g, Protein: 6 g, Fiber:18 g

Dinner: Coconut Cabbage Stew

Preparation time: 10 minutes
Cooking time: 15 minutes
Servings: 2

Ingredients
2 tablespoons of olive oil
1 red onion, peeled and chopped
Salt and black pepper, to taste
2 large cloves of garlic, diced
1 teaspoon red chili powder
½ tablespoon mustard seeds
½ tablespoon curry powder
½ tablespoon turmeric powder
3 cups cabbage, quartered and shredded
½ cup carrot, peeled and sliced
4 tablespoons lemon juice
2 cups unsweetened coconut milk
½ cup water

Ingredients For The Topping
1 cup almond and cream, topping
Side serving
2 servings of steamed brown rice

Directions
Take a skillet and heat olive oil in it. Cook the onions, in it for 1 minute, and add garlic.
Once you can smell it, add salt, mustard seeds, curry powder, turmeric powder, and red chili powder. Mix well, and add all the remaining ingredients excluding, coconut milk, and topping. Cook covered for 10 minutes.
Afterward pour coconut milk and simmer for a few minutes. Once it's done, serve with the topping of cashew cream.
Serve it with your favorite plant-based side dish.

Nutritional Facts Per Serving:
Calories: 280, Fat: 10 g, Carbs: 18 g, Protein: 8 g, Fiber:12 g

Dessert: Fat Bombs

Preparation time: 10 minutes
Servings: 2

Ingredients
1-1/2 cups shredded coconut flakes
1/4 cup organic nut butter
Pinch of cinnamon
¼ teaspoon of vanilla extract

Directions
Take a skillet and heat it over a medium pan.
Roast the coconut flakes in the pan and then add nut butter, cinnamon, and vanilla extract.
Transfer the mixture to the bowl and mix all the ingredients by hand and make small candy sized balls.
Refrigerate for a few minutes. Once it's solid, serve.

Nutritional Facts Per Serving:
Calories: 340, Fat: 20 g, Carbs: 10 g, Protein: 10 g, Fiber:2 g

DAY 12

Breakfast: Savory Cauliflower Bread

Preparation time: 10 minutes
Cooking time: 20 minutes
Servings: 2-3

Ingredients
2 cups almond flour
1 very ripe banana
4 tablespoons of flaxseed
1 cup of cauliflower florets, grated
1 cup of soy milk
4 tablespoons of vegetable butter, melted
Pinch of salt

Directions
Use a food processor to grate the cauliflower, then add almond flour, flax seed.
Then add liquid ingredients including butter, and soy milk.
Mash banana in a bowl and add it to the blender. Add pinch of salt and pulse the ingredients.
Oil greased loaf pan and pour the mixture in it. Pour 1 cup water in instant pot and adjust trivet on top. Make a sling of the aluminum foil and place it on trivet. Put the loaf pan on top of the trivet. Lock the lid of the instant pot and cook for 20 minutes, at high pressure. Once the timer beeps, release the steam naturally. Let it put it on a cooling rack.
Once cool serve. Enjoy.

Nutritional Facts Per Serving:
Calories: 290, Fat: 6 g, Carbs: 28 g, Protein: 4 g, Fiber:8 g

Lunch: Pasta Salad

Preparation time: 10 minutes
Cooking time: 20 minutes
Servings: 4

Ingredients

10 ounces penne pasta
8 ounces of green beans
1 tablespoon of olive oil
1 cup jalapeño, chopped
1 tablespoon of minced garlic
2 cherry tomatoes
½ cup dry white wine vinegar
Salt and black pepper, to taste
2 tablespoons of fresh thyme

Directions

Cook pasta according to package instruction. When only 5 minutes remain, add green beans and reserve 1 cup of water from the pasta, for further use. Drain pasta and green beans.
Take a skillet and add oil in it. Cook it for 5 minutes. Next, add garlic to the skillet and add tomatoes. Cook until juice comes out. Now, pour wine and cook until it evaporates.
Add pasta, green beans, and jalapeños. Pour in the reserved water. Add seasoning and thyme. Cook for 10 minutes, or until the liquid evaporates. Then serve and enjoy.

Nutritional Facts Per Serving:

Calories: 450, Fat: 6 g, Carbs: 40 g, Protein: 4 g, Fiber:9 g

Dinner: Zucchini-Mushroom Bowl

Preparation time: 10 minutes
Cooking time: 18 minutes
Servings: 4

Ingredients
2 medium zucchinis
Salt and black pepper, as needed
3 tablespoons of olive oil
1 cup onion
4 garlic cloves, minced
1 cup cremini mushrooms, chopped
1 tablespoon of tomato paste
1 cup tomatoes, chopped and fried
6 ounces fresh baby spinach, chopped
½ cup fresh basil, chopped

Directions
Take a vegetable peeler and peel the zucchini. Toss the salt and black pepper onto the zucchini. Take a Dutch oven and heat oil in it over medium flame. Add garlic and onion and cook for 5 minutes. Next, add mushroom and cook for 5 minutes. Add tomato paste, tomatoes, pepper and salt. Reduce the heat to medium and simmer occasionally.
Then add in striped zucchinis and baby spinach. Sprinkle basil at the end. Serve and enjoy.

Nutritional Facts Per Serving:
Calories: 360, Fat: 6 g, Carbs: 30 g, Protein: 4 g, Fiber:12 g

Snack: Herbed Potato Hummus

Preparation time: 10 minutes
Servings: 6

Ingredients
1 cup of basil leaves
3 cups of garbanzo beans
1 cup vegetable broth
½ cup parsley leaves, lightly packed
¼ cup lemon juice, squeezed
4 tablespoons sesame seeds, toasted
3 cloves garlic
1 cup chopped chives
2 baked potatoes

Directions
Chop all the listed ingredients in a blender, excluding baked potatoes. Once the smooth consistency is achieved, serve it on a baked potato.

Nutritional Facts Per Serving:
Calories: 280, Fat: 9 g, Carbs: 30 g, Protein: 8 g, Fiber:10 g

DAY 13

Breakfast: Raspberry Truffle Brownies

Preparation time: 10 minutes
Cooking time: 15 minutes
Servings: 4

Ingredients
6 ounces unsweetened chocolate, chopped
1/3 cup raspberry jam
½ cup of cane sugar
1/3 cup unsweetened applesauce
1 teaspoon pure vanilla extract
¼ teaspoon almond extract
1-1/2 cups whole wheat pastry flour
½ cup unsweetened cocoa powder
¼ teaspoon baking powder
½ teaspoon baking soda
¼ teaspoon salt
1-1/2 cup raspberries, frozen or fresh

Directions
Preheat the oven to 375 degrees F. Line a parchment paper baking dish. Take a bowl and melt chocolate in it. Take a bowl and mix all the dry ingredient.
In another bowl, add all the wet ingredients. Mix all the ingredients well. Fold and mix the ingredients of both the bowls.
Spread this mixture into the prepared pan. Bake the brownies in preheated oven for 15 minutes. Once done, take out to let it get cool. Serve.

Nutritional Facts Per Serving:
Calories: 280, Fat: 4 g, Carbs: 30 g, Protein: 6 g, Fiber:12 g

Lunch: Broccoli Lemon Pasta

Preparation time: 10 minutes
Cooking time: 30 minutes
Servings: 3

Ingredients
1 pound of broccoli crowns
1/3 cup of vegetable oil
1 lemon, sliced
6 ounces of whole grain shell pasta
2 tablespoons of vegetable butter
2 garlic cloves, minced
1/4 teaspoon red pepper
3/4 teaspoon salt
1/2 teaspoon black pepper
2 teaspoons lemon zest

Directions
Preheat the oven to 450 degrees F. Toss chopped broccoli with oil. Layer broccoli in a baking dish. Arrange lemon in the side. Bake it in the oven for 15 minutes until tender. In a Dutch oven bring the water to the boil. Cook the pasta according to package instructions in the Dutch oven. Drain and reserve the pasta liquid. Now remove the pasta from the Dutch oven and dry the Dutch oven with a paper towel. Heat it at medium flame and then cook the butter until browned and fragrant, about 3 minutes.

Add the garlic and red peppers. Stir generously. Then add in pasta and season it with salt and black pepper. Add reserved liquid and broccoli. Cook for 10 more minutes until liquid evaporates. Top with lemon zest and enjoy.

Nutritional Facts Per Serving:
Calories: 480, Fat: 4 g, Carbs: 48 g, Protein: 4 g, Fiber:10 g

Dinner: Sweet Potato Soup

Preparation time: 10 minutes
Cooking time: 55 minutes
Servings: 3

Ingredients
1 large sweet potato
2 cups of vegetable broth
½ cup of almond milk
2 garlic cloves
1 teaspoon of chipotle powder
1 teaspoon of lime juice

Ingredients For The Topping
1 avocado, pitted
1 cup corn chips
Dash of smoky paprika
1 tablespoon of lime juice

Directions
Preheat the oven to 430 degrees F. Pierce sweet potatoes and bake in oven for 55 minutes.
Peel off the skin of potatoes and set aside for further use. In a blender, pulse together milk, broth, potato flesh, garlic, lime, and chipotle powder.
Adjust the seasoning by adding salt and black pepper. Now pour the soup into a cooking pot, and simmer at low heat. Once hot serve into serving bowls. Top with all the toppings.

Nutritional Facts Per Serving:
Calories: 380, Fat: 6 g, Carbs: 40 g, Protein: 4 g, Fiber:8 g

Snack: Raw Broccoli Poppers

Preparation time: 10 minutes
Cooking time: 7 Hours (Dehydrate)
Servings: 2

Ingredients
2 cups broccoli florets, washed and chopped
½ cup cashews, soaked overnight
½ red bell pepper, chopped and seeds removed
2 tablespoons lemon juice, squeezed
1/6 cup water
2 teaspoons of nutritional yeast
1/2 teaspoon of onion powder
½ teaspoon of turmeric powder
Salt and black pepper, to taste

Directions
Take a high-speed blender and pulse cashews in it. Take a container and chop red bell peppers in it. Then add lemon juice, nutritional yeast, water, onion powder, salt, and turmeric powder. Process it for 45 seconds. Take a bowl and place broccoli in it. Add container mixture and then cashew cream. Mix it and coat broccoli well with the mixture.
Dehydrate at 125 degrees F for 7 hours. Once, it's crunchy take out the broccoli.
Serve and enjoy.

Nutritional Facts Per Serving:
Calories: 250, Fat: 4 g, Carbs: 24 g, Protein: 8 g, Fiber:15 g

DAY 14

Breakfast: Lemon Muffins

Preparation time: 10 minutes
Cooking time: 25 minutes
Servings: 4

Ingredients
10 tablespoons of warm water
4 tablespoons of ground flaxseed
½ teaspoon vanilla extract
3 cups gluten-free flour, all-purpose
½ teaspoon baking soda
salt to taste
½ cup almond milk
1/3 cup maple syrup
1/4 cup coconut oil
2 teaspoons lemon zest, finely grated
½ tablespoon lemon juice
1/4 cup chia seeds

Directions
Preheat the oven to 375 degrees F. Line a muffin tray with muffin cups. Take a bowl, and mix water, flaxseed, and set it aside for soaking. In a separate bowl, mix lemon juice, maple syrup, vanilla, oil, lemon zest, milk, and beat it until smooth. Then add soaked flaxseeds, and use a spatula to mix it well. Now, combine baking soda, flour, salt, and chia seeds. Mix it into a smooth paste. Pour the batter into muffin cups and sprinkle chia seeds on top.
Bake in the oven for 25 minutes. Let it sit for 10 minutes before serving. Enjoy.

Nutritional Facts Per Serving:
Calories: 310, Fat: 7 g, Carbs: 40 g, Protein: 4 g, Fiber:6 g

Lunch: Tofu Chow Mein

Preparation time: 10 minutes
Cooking time: 7 minutes
Servings: 4

Ingredients
10 ounces whole-wheat angel hair pasta, uncooked
4 tablespoons sesame oil, divided
20 ounces of extra-firm tofu
1-1/2 cups sliced fresh mushrooms
2 sweet red peppers, julienned
1/2 cup reduced-sodium soy sauce
4 green onions, thinly sliced

Directions
Take a large cooking pot and cook the pasta in boiling water, according to package instructions.
In a skillet, heat the oil and cook onions for 2 minutes.
Then add mushrooms, pepper, and tofu. Then add cooked and drained pasta and stir fry mushrooms, pepper, and tofu.
Simmer it for 5 minutes.
In the end, add soy sauce and serve.

Nutritional Facts Per Serving:
Calories: 340, Fat: 6 g, Carbs: 38 g, Protein: 8 g, Fiber:10 g

Dinner: Vegan Tacos

Preparation time: 10 minutes
Cooking time: 20 minutes
Servings: 3

Ingredients
6 tortillas
1 cup refried beans
4 cups Portobello mushrooms, chopped
2 red bell peppers, chopped
1 onion, chopped

Chipotle Marinade
1 tablespoon sesame oil
2 tablespoons chipotle in adobo sauce
1 minced garlic clove, minced
¼ teaspoon cumin
¼ teaspoon coriander
Salt and black pepper, to taste

Toppings
½ cup pickled onions
1 avocado, pitted

Directions
Preheat the oven to 375 degrees F. Slice the bell pepper and mushrooms in thick wedges. Also, cut the onions in half-moons. Place the ingredients in a sheet pan lined with a baking sheet.
Next, mix all the marinade ingredients in a bowl and brush the mushroom, red bell pepper, and onions with marinade. Roast it for 20 minutes until tender.
Warm the tortilla and then spread refried beans on top.
Divide the oven mixture on top equally and then top it with fresh avocados and pickled onions.

Nutritional Facts Per Serving:
Calories: 380, Fat: 8 g, Carbs: 35 g, Protein: 10 g, Fiber:18 g

Snack: Strawberry-Mango Ice

Preparation time: 10 minutes
Servings: 4

Ingredients
3 cups sugar, divided
1 quart strawberries, diced
1 cup mango juice
1 cup toasted coconut

Directions
Take a medium pot and bring water to boil about a cup.
Dissolve sugar in it. Remove it from heat and add 2 cups of water. Pour the mixture in a baking dish and freeze for 5 hours.
Stir it every 45 minutes.
Now, in a blender process the strawberries and remaining sugar. Transfer it to a container and pour mango juice in it. Divide the ice into four serving glasses and divide the strawberry mixture and mango juice on top of each.
Enjoy.

Nutritional Facts Per Serving:
Calories: 230, Fat: 8 g, Carbs: 28 g, Protein: 10 g, Fiber:4 g

DAY 15

Breakfast: Zucchini bread with pistachios and fennel

Preparation time: 50 minutes
Cooking time: 15 minutes
Servings: 4

Ingredients
1/4 cup of raw chopped pistachios
3 tablespoons of coconut oil
1 tablespoon of apple cedar vinegar
1/4 cup of plan dairy free yoghurt
2 teaspoons of fennel seeds
1/2 teaspoon of salt
1 teaspoon of baking soda
1 teaspoon of baking powder
1/4 cup of tapioca starch
1/2 cup of almond flour
3/4 cup of brown rice flour
1 cup of quinoa flour
1 cup of sugar
6 teaspoons of hot water
2 teaspoons of ground flax seeds
1 pound of yellow summer squash and zucchinis

Directions
Line the bottom of a four and a half inch by eight-and-a-half-inch loaf pan with flour. Preheat oven to 350f. Using the larger holes of the grater, shred the yellow squash and zucchini and let the mixture drain in a strainer for half an hour.
While the mixture drains, combine the hot water with the flax seeds and set it aside to slur.
Dry the zucchini mixture in paper towels by squeezing it. In a bowl, mix it with apple cedar vinegar, and the plain yoghurt. Whisk the coconut oil together with the sugar in a mixing bowl. Include the flux slurry and combine it.
Combine half of the zucchini with half of the flour mixture; keep adding both as you mix, until you finish both mixtures. Into the baking pan include the batter and top it with the remainder of the pistachios and let it bake for one hour. Cool it for a quarter of an hour before moving it into a cooling rack.
You can have it warm or let it cool completely, alternatively let it sit in the fridge overnight to flavor and eat it in a maximum of two days.

Nutritional Facts Per Serving:
Calories: 360, Fat: 7 g, Carbs: 24 g, Protein: 9 g, Fiber:6 g

Lunch: Cashew Siam Salad

Preparation time: 10 minutes
Cooking time: 3 minutes
Servings: 4

Ingredients For The Salad
4 cups baby spinach, rinsed, drained
½ cup pickled red cabbage

Ingredients For The Dressing
1-inch piece ginger, finely chopped
1 teaspoon chili garlic paste
1 tablespoon soy sauce
½ tablespoon rice vinegar
1 tablespoon sesame oil
3 tablespoon avocado oil

Ingredients For The Toppings
½ cup raw cashews, unsalted
¼ cup fresh cilantro, chopped (optional)

Directions
Put the spinach and red cabbage in a large bowl. Toss to combine and set the salad aside.
Toast the cashews in a frying pan over medium-high heat, stirring occasionally until the cashews are golden brown. This should take about 3 minutes. Turn off the heat and set the frying pan aside.
Mix all the dressing ingredients in a medium-sized bowl and use a spoon to mix them into a smooth dressing. Pour the dressing over the spinach salad and top with the toasted cashews.
Toss the salad to combine all ingredients and transfer the large bowl to the fridge.
Allow the salad to chill for up to one hour – doing so will guarantee a better flavor. Alternatively, the salad can be served right away, topped with the optional cilantro. Enjoy!

Nutritional Facts Per Serving:
Calories: 340, Fat: 7 g, Carbs: 40 g, Protein: 4 g, Fiber: 4 g

Dinner: Chickpea, Mango and Curried Cauliflower Salad

Preparation time: 10 minutes
Cooking time: 32 minutes
Servings: 4

Ingredients
1 teaspoon curry powder
1 teaspoon sugar
1 teaspoon ground mustard
1 teaspoon ground coriander
½ teaspoon ground turmeric
½ teaspoon ground cumin
3 tablespoons olive oil more as needed
1 medium yellow onion thinly sliced
1 cup canned chickpeas drained, rinsed and warmed through slightly
1 head of cauliflower cut into 1-inch florets, blanch for 2 minutes in boiling water and then pat dry
2 large mangoes peeled, pitted and chopped into ½-inch pieces
1 jalapeño stemmed, seeded and diced small
1 cup chopped cilantro
2 tablespoons lime juice
2 cups baby spinach
1 cup baby arugula
Salt and black pepper

Directions
Blend the curry powder, cinnamon, ground mustard, coriander, cumin, ½ teaspoon of salt, and ¼ teaspoon black pepper in a small bowl. Set it aside.
Put the olive oil in a large skillet. Add the onion and cook at high heat for about 6 minutes. Sprinkle in the spices and turn the heat to medium-low. Cook an extra 6 minutes.
Move to a wide bowl and add to the same bowl as the chickpeas. Keep the pan at medium heat.
Add the cauliflower to the same pan where the onion was cooked. If required, add more olive oil. Cook in the remaining spice mixture for about 5 minutes or until the cauliflower is seasoned and cooked. Use the onion and chickpeas to transfer the cauliflower to the bowl.
Let sit for approximately 20 minutes at room temperature.
Apply the pineapple, jalapeño, coriander, lime juice, spinach, and arugula to the dish. Toss in order to disperse the ingredients evenly. Adjust seasoning to taste and serve as soon as possible. Enjoy!

Nutritional Facts Per Serving:
Calories: 350, Fat: 6 g, Carbs: 20 g, Protein: 5 g, Fiber:18 g

Dessert: Double Chocolate Cupcakes

Preparation time: 10 minutes
Cooking time: 25 minutes
Servings: 4

Ingredients
2.5 ounces chocolate, nondairy and unsweetened
1-1/2 cups unsweetened almond milk
1 teaspoon apple cider vinegar
⅔ Cup dry maple sugar
1/3 cup unsweetened applesauce
½ teaspoon pure vanilla extract
1-1/2 cups spelt flour
1/3 cup cocoa powder, unsweetened
1/4 teaspoon baking soda
1 teaspoon baking powder
Salt, pinch

Directions
Preheat the oven to 375 degrees F. Line a muffin tray with muffin cups. In a bowl melt chocolate, using the microwave. Set it aside. Take a large bowl and combine milk and apple cider vinegar. Set aside for a few minutes.
Once curdled, add maple sugar, vanilla, chocolate, and applesauce. Take a separate bowl and add flour, baking soda, cocoa powder, baking powder, and salt.
Add wet ingredients into the dry ingredients and combine ingredients of both the bowls. Mix until no lumps remain. Scoop this batter to the muffins tray. Bake for 25 minutes. Remove the muffins afterward and put them on a cooling rack. Serve and enjoy.

Nutritional Facts Per Serving:
Calories: 310, Fat: 10 g, Carbs: 36 g, Protein: 6 g, Fiber:3 g

DAY 16

Breakfast: Zucchini quinoa peas pancakes
Preparation time: 10 minutes
Cooking time: 10 minutes
Servings: 3

Ingredients (for ten pancakes)
A quarter teaspoon of salt
A tablespoon of salt
Half cup of quinoa flour
A teaspoon of olive oil
A tablespoon of vanilla extract
Two ripe bananas
A whole zucchini
A cupful of green peas

Directions:
Process the olive oil, vanilla extract, bananas, zucchini and the green peas in a food processor.
Thoroughly mix the salt, baking powder and quinoa flour in a bowl.
Combine the zucchini mixture with the flour mixture. Heat and grease a non-sticky pan.
Cook by spooning one and a half teaspoons of the mixture into the pan into a circular shape.
When well done on one side, flip and cook the other. Repeating this process for the whole batter.

Nutritional Facts Per Serving:
Calories: 280, Fat: 6 g, Carbs: 20 g, Protein: 9 g, Fiber:12 g

Lunch: Butternut Squash Tacos with Tempeh Chorizo

Preparation time: 10 minutes
Cooking time: 40 minutes
Servings: 5

Ingredients:
One 8-ounce package tempeh
½ cup of filtered water
¼ cup apple cider vinegar
2 cups butternut squash, peeled, cut into cubes
1 teaspoon chili powder
½ teaspoon smoked paprika
½ teaspoon cumin
½ teaspoon garlic powder
½ teaspoon oregano
A dash of cayenne
1 tablespoon nutritional yeast
A few dashes of liquid smoke
Black pepper and sea salt to taste
½ cup thinly julienned carrot (optional)
8 corn tortillas (or whatever you have on hand)
1 large avocado, pitted and sliced
Cilantro, chopped

Directions
Cut the tempeh into two parts. Steam for 10 min. Place in a large bowl and tear apart into small pieces either with your hands (after it's cooled) or with a pastry cutter.
While tempeh is steaming, bring water and vinegar to a boil in a small skillet. Add spices, squash, liquid smoke, nutritional yeast, and a pinch of sea salt to skillet. Coat well and simmer covered, stirring occasionally.
Add carrots and tempeh, covering again. Simmer a little while longer, stirring to prevent sticking. Uncover and season with pepper and salt. Fill warmed tortillas with squash and tempeh mix and top with avocado and cilantro.

Nutritional Facts Per Serving:
Calories: 380, Fat: 7 g, Carbs: 25 g, Protein: 8 g, Fiber:13 g

Dinner: Healthy Lentil Soup

Preparation time: 10 minutes
Cooking time: 20 minutes
Servings: 6

Ingredients
1 ½ teaspoons vegetable oil
2 medium carrots, sliced
1 ½ onions, chopped
1 ½ cups dry brown lentils, rinsed, soaked for about 2 hours
3 bay leaves
2 tablespoons lemon juice or to taste
6 cups vegetable broth
½ teaspoon dried thyme
Salt to taste
Pepper to taste

Directions
Place a soup pot over medium heat. Add oil. When the oil is heated, add onions and sauté until translucent. Add the rest of the ingredients except lemon juice and stir. When it begins to boil, lower the heat and cover with a lid. Simmer until the lentils are tender.
Add lemon juice and stir. Ladle into soup bowls and serve.

Nutritional Facts Per Serving:
Calories: 250, Fat: 6 g, Carbs: 20 g, Protein: 18 g, Fiber:16 g

Dessert: Lemony Oats Cookies

Preparation time: 10 minutes
Cooking time: 35 minutes
Servings: 4

Ingredients
12 dates, pitted
1/3 cup unsweetened applesauce
2 teaspoons apple cider vinegar
1-1/2 cup rolled oats
1 cup oat flour
¼ cup quick-cooking oats
½ cup roughly chopped walnuts
1 tablespoon lemon zest
4 teaspoons cocoa powder, natural
1 teaspoon vanilla powder
1 teaspoon baking soda
Salt, pinch

Directions
Preheat the oven to 300 degrees F. Line a baking sheet with parchment paper.
Take a bowl, and add dates and cover it with hot water. Let the dates soak for one hour.
Drain the water and take out the date. Transfer the dates to a blender and add applesauce, vinegar, and blend. Set aside the paste.
Take a separate bowl and add oats, flour, and quick-cooking oats, lemon zest, walnuts, vanilla powder, baking soda, salt, and cocoa powder. Add the date mix to the flour mixture. Mix well. Use a wooden spatula to mix the ingredients. Scoop a golf-sized ball of batter on to the flat surface and flatten with hands.
Place these cookies onto a baking pan. Bake in the oven for 35 minutes. Once cooked transfer it to the baking rack and let it get cool at room temperature. Once it's done, serve.

Nutritional Facts Per Serving:
Calories: 290, Fat: 4 g, Carbs: 35 g, Protein: 4 g, Fiber:8 g

DAY 17

Breakfast: Banana chocolate chip muffins

Preparation time: 10 minutes
Cooking time: 45 minutes
Servings: 4

Ingredients
2.47 oz of chocolate chips
Two tablespoon of caramel extract
1.4 oz sunflower oil
5 oz of ripe bananas
6.35 oz of the nondairy milk of choice
Half teaspoon of baking powder
3.5 oz of sugar
9.17 oz of self-rising flour

Directions
Combine the flour and baking powder in a bowl
Preheat oven to 356f. Combine the oil and milk in a bowl and whip it thoroughly. Include the sugar in the oil/milk mixture and combine well. Combine the mixture well.
Mash the bananas and include them in the wet mixture. Combine with the flour by including it in portions as you mix till all the flour is gone.
Include the chocolate chips in the mixture.
For 45 minutes bake the mixture in muffin tins until golden.
To see if they are ready, test them using a toothpick. If the toothpick comes out clean, they are ready to serve.

Nutritional Facts Per Serving:
Calories: 320, Fat: 7 g, Carbs: 38 g, Protein: 4 g, Fiber:4 g

Lunch: Avocado and Cauliflower Hummus

Preparation time: 10 minutes + 30 minutes
Cooking time: 20/25 minutes
Servings: 2

Ingredients
1 medium cauliflower, stem removed and chopped
1 large Hass avocado, peeled, pitted, and chopped
¼ cup extra virgin olive oil
2 garlic cloves
½ tablespoon lemon juice
½ teaspoon onion powder
Sea salt and ground black pepper to taste
2 large carrots
¼ cup fresh cilantro, chopped (optional)

Directions
Preheat the oven to 450°F, and line a baking tray with aluminum foil. Put the chopped cauliflower on the baking tray and drizzle with 2 tablespoons of olive oil.
Roast the chopped cauliflower in the oven for 20-25 minutes, until lightly brown. Remove the tray from the oven and allow the cauliflower to cool down.
Add all the ingredients—except the carrots and optional fresh cilantro—to a food processor or blender, and blend the ingredients into a smooth hummus.
Transfer the hummus to a medium-sized bowl, cover, and put it in the fridge for at least 30 minutes.
Take the hummus out of the fridge and, if desired, top it with the optional chopped cilantro and more salt and pepper to taste; serve with the carrot fries, and enjoy!

Nutritional Facts Per Serving:
Calories: 390, Fat: 10 g, Carbs: 28 g, Protein: 10 g, Fiber:12 g

Dinner: Roasted Vegetables and Lentil Salad

Preparation time: 10 minutes
Cooking time: 45 minutes
Servings: 2

Ingredients
2 cups butternut squash (cubed)
2 cups Brussels sprouts (quartered)
1 red onion (cut in wedges)
1 tablespoon olive oil
Salt, to taste
Pepper, to taste
1 cup green lentils (rinsed)
3 cups water or vegetable broth
3 tablespoons balsamic vinegar
1 tablespoon maple syrup

Directions
Start by preheating the oven by setting the temperature to 400 degrees Fahrenheit. Take a baking dish and line it with parchment paper. Toss in the butternut squash, red onions and Brussels sprouts. Generously season with salt, pepper and olive oil. Mix well using your hands and ensure all ingredients are well coated. Place the tray in the baking tray in the oven and bake for 10 minutes. Flip the veggies and bake for another 10 minutes.

Take a medium nonstick saucepan and place it over high flame. Add in the water/vegetable broth and lentils. Once it comes to a boil, cover the pan with a lid and let it simmer for about 25 minutes. Drain any excess water and keep aside. Take a large mixing bowl and empty the roasted vegetables. Also transfer the cooked lentils to the mixing bowl.

To prepare the dressing, take a liquid measuring cup and add in the balsamic vinegar, pepper, salt and maple syrup. Whisk well to combine. Pour the prepared dressing over roasted vegetables and lentil. Toss well to make sure all ingredients are well coated. Transfer into 2 bowls and serve.

Nutritional Facts Per Serving:
Calories: 420, Fat: 8 g, Carbs: 38 g, Protein: 12 g, Fiber:14 g

Dessert: Raspberry Brownies

Preparation time: 10 minutes
Cooking time: 20 minutes
Servings: 4/5

Ingredients
1 cup raspberry jam, organic and all-natural
6 ounces of chocolate, unsweetened and chopped
1 cup of cane sugar
1 cup of applesauce
1 teaspoon of vanilla extract
¼ teaspoon almond extract
2 cups whole wheat pastry flour
1/3 cup unsweetened cocoa powder
1 teaspoon baking powder
1 teaspoon baking soda
1/6 teaspoon salt
½ cup raspberries, frozen

Directions
Preheat the oven to 375 degrees F. Line a baking sheet over a baking pan. Take a bowl and melt chocolate in it by placing it in the microwave, for a few seconds.
Take a large bowl and mix applesauce, jam, sweetener, vanilla, also extract and melted chocolate. Mix it very well. Now stir in flour, baking powder, baking soda, salt, and cocoa powder. At the end fold in the raspberries. Mix well and spread the mixture into the baking pan lined with parchment paper. Bake it in the oven for 20 minutes. Once done remove it from the oven and let it sit on the cooling rack. Once it's cool, serve by slicing in to brownie shapes.

Nutritional Facts Per Serving:
Calories: 340, Fat: 7 g, Carbs: 50 g, Protein: 4 g, Fiber:4 g

DAY 18

Breakfast: Cardamom persimmon scones with maple cream

Preparation time: 20 minutes
Cooking time: 20 minutes
Servings: 4

Ingredients For The Maple Cream
1/4 teaspoon of salt
1/4 teaspoon of cinnamon
1 tablespoon of maple syrup
3/4 cup of non dairy milk
2 tablespoons of shredded coconut
1/2 cup of persimmons chopped Scones
The wet ingredients
1 cup of chopped fuyu persimmons.
1 teaspoon of vanilla extract
1 teaspoon of apple cedar vinegar
1/2 cup of almond milk
1 cup of plain vegan yoghurt
The dry ingredients
3 tablespoons of soft coconut oil
1/2 tablespoon of salt
1/2 tablespoon of cinnamon
1 teaspoon of cardamom
2 teaspoons of baking powder
1 tablespoon of coconut sugar
2 cups of all-purpose flour

Directions for preparing the cream.
Blend all the cream ingredients in a blender. Good with the scones when warm. You can have it in the fridge for up to 2 days.

Directions for the scones
Line a baking sheet on the oven with parchment. Preheat oven to 400f. Put together the salt, spices, baking soda, sugar, and flour in a mixing bowl. Mix the components evenly. Add coconut oil into the mixture. Whisk the vanilla, apple cedar vinegar, almond milk, and yoghurt in a bowl. Carefully mix in the dry and wet ingredients till well combined without overdoing it. Using a wooden spoon, fold in the chopped persimmons.
On a flat firm surface, sprinkle some flour and bring the dough into a round shape of not more than an inch thickness. Divide it into eight wedges separate wedges and transfer them into the preset baking sheet. Let them cook for a maximum of 20 minutes and let it cool down. It is now ready to serve along with the cream.

Nutritional Facts Per Serving:
Calories: 340, Fat: 10 g, Carbs: 30 g, Protein: 4 g, Fiber:6 g

Lunch: Raw Zoodles with Avocado 'N Nuts

Preparation time: 10 minutes
Servings: 2

Ingredients
1 medium zucchini
1½ cups basil
1/3 cup water
5 tablespoons pine nuts
2 tablespoons lemon juice
1 medium avocado, peeled, pitted, sliced
Optional: 2 tablespoons olive oil
6 yellow cherry tomatoes, halved
Optional: 6 red cherry tomatoes, halved
Sea salt and black pepper to taste

Directions
Add the basil, water, nuts, lemon juice, avocado slices, olive oil (if desired), salt, and pepper to a blender.
Blend the ingredients into a smooth mixture. Add more salt and pepper to taste and blend again. Divide the sauce and the zucchini noodles between two medium-sized bowls for serving, and combine in each.
Top the mixtures with the halved yellow cherry tomatoes, and the optional red cherry tomatoes (if desired); serve and enjoy!

Nutritional Facts Per Serving:
Calories: 320, Fat: 12 g, Carbs: 18 g, Protein: 10 g, Fiber:12 g

Dinner: Spicy SunDried Tomato Soup with White Beans & Swiss Chard

Preparation time: 10 minutes
Cooking time: 10 minutes
Servings: 4

Ingredients
1 tablespoon olive oil
¼ teaspoon red pepper flakes
1 medium carrot, sliced
½ small zucchini, sliced
¾ cup chopped onion
1 stalk celery, chopped
1 teaspoon minced fresh rosemary
1 can (15 ounces) diced tomatoes
¼ cup oil-packed sundried tomatoes, drained, chopped
1 tablespoon oil from oil packed sun-drained tomatoes
¼ teaspoon chopped thyme
2 cloves garlic, minced
1 cup vegetable broth
½ can (from a 15 ounces can) white beans or cannellini beans, rinsed, drained
3 ounces Swiss chard, chopped
½ cup torn basil

Directions
Place a soup pot over medium heat. Add oil. When the oil is heated, add garlic and red pepper flakes and sauté until aromatic. Add onion, carrots, zucchini, celery, and rosemary and sauté until onions turn translucent. Stir in the broth, beans, and ½ can tomatoes. Mix well.
Add some of the mixture into the blender. Add rest of the canned tomatoes, sundried tomatoes, and its oil and blend until smooth. Pour it back into the pot. Heat thoroughly. Add salt and pepper to taste. Let it simmer for a few minutes. Garnish with basil and serve. Ladle into soup bowls.

Nutritional Facts Per Serving:
Calories: 250, Fat: 6 g, Carbs: 20 g, Protein: 6 g, Fiber:14 g

Dessert: Plant-Based Mug Cake

Preparation time: 5 minutes
Cooking time: 2 minutes
Servings: 1

Ingredients
6 tablespoons of spelt flour
5 tablespoons of cocoa powder
1 scoop stevia
4 teaspoons of pumpkin puree
6 tablespoons cashew milk, unsweetened

Directions
Take a large microwave-safe mug and mix all the ingredients in it. Mix until smooth texture obtained. Place it in the microwave and cook for 2 minutes at a high temperature. Serve.

Nutritional Facts Per Serving:
Calories: 270, Fat: 3 g, Carbs: 20 g, Protein: 6 g, Fiber: 4 g

DAY 19

Breakfast: Quinoa crepes

Preparation time: 10 minutes
Cooking time: 15 minutes
Servings: 1

Ingredients
Vegan butter oil or, if you prefer, coconut oil spray
2 teaspoons of vanilla extract
3 tablespoons of maple syrup
1-1/2 tablespoon of ground flax seeds
4-1/2 cups of almond milk
3 cups of quinoa flour

Directions
If your flax seeds are not ground, grind them in a blender (high speed). Whisk the ingredients together in a bowl till they smoothen.
On medium heat in a crepe pan, heat some coconut oil. Let your pan heat up first. Apply a thin layer of the batter on your pan in a round shape.
Cook until a brown color appears on the edges.
When it's easily coming off the pan, flip on the other side and let it cook as well. Do the same for the remaining batter.
You can serve with the topping of your choice. Try out vegan nutella and fresh berries if you like.

Nutritional Facts Per Serving:
Calories: 300, Fat: 9 g, Carbs: 30 g, Protein: 6 g, Fiber:4 g

Lunch: Spicy Black Bean Soup

Preparation time: 10 minutes
Cooking time: 15 minutes
Servings: 4

Ingredients

1 large onion, finely chopped
2 tablespoons olive oil
2 jalapeño peppers, deseeded, minced
2 red bell peppers, chopped
2 cups vegetable broth
3 teaspoons freshly ground cumin
2 tablespoons balsamic vinegar
1 Hungarian pepper, deseeded, minced
4 cloves garlic, minced
2 cans (15 ounces each) black beans
1 avocado, peeled, pitted, chopped
Salt to taste
Pepper to taste
2 tablespoons fresh cilantro, chopped (optional)
4 tortillas

Directions

Mash about one can of black beans. Add garlic to it and stir. Set aside. Place a heavy-bottomed pot over medium heat.
Add oil. When the oil is heated, add onions, peppers (all the varieties) and cumin and sauté until the vegetables are soft. Add rest of the ingredients except cilantro and bring to a boil.
Ladle into soup bowls and serve hot garnished with cilantro.

Nutritional Facts Per Serving:

Calories: 340, Fat: 7 g, Carbs: 40 g, Protein: 4 g, Fiber:4 g

Dinner: Cauliflower Sushi

Preparation time: 30 minutes
Servings: 4

Ingredients For The Sushi Base
6 cups cauliflower florets
½ cup vegan cheese
1 medium spring onion, diced
4 nori sheets
Sea salt and pepper to taste
1 tablespoon rice vinegar or sushi vinegar
1 medium garlic clove, minced

Ingredients For The Filling
1 medium Hass avocado, peeled, sliced
½ medium cucumber, skinned, sliced
4 asparagus spears
A handful of enoki mushrooms

Directions
Put the cauliflower florets in a food processor or blender. Pulse the florets into a rice-like substance. When using readymade cauliflower rice, add this to the blender. Add the vegan cheese, spring onions, and vinegar to the food processor or blender.
Top these ingredients with salt and pepper to taste, and pulse everything into a chunky mixture. Make sure not to turn the ingredients into a puree by pulsing too long.
Taste and add more vinegar, salt, or pepper to taste. Add the optional minced garlic clove to the blender and pulse again for a few seconds.
Lay out the nori sheets and spread the cauliflower rice mixture out evenly between the sheets. Make sure to leave at least 2 inches of the top and bottom edges empty.
Place one or more combinations of multiple filling ingredients along the center of the spread out rice mixture. Experiment with different ingredients per nori sheet for the best flavor.
Roll up each nori sheet tightly. (Using a sushi mat will make this easier). Either serve the sushi as a nori roll, or, slice each roll up into sushi pieces. Serve right away with a small amount of wasabi, pickled ginger, and soy sauce.

Nutritional Facts Per Serving:
Calories: 320, Fat: 7 g, Carbs: 30 g, Protein: 8 g, Fiber:19 g

Dessert: Quinoa Pudding

Preparation time: 10 minutes
Cooking time: 18 minutes
Servings: 2

Ingredients
1 cup quinoa, pre-soaked
1 cup almond milk
3 cups of water
1 scoop of stevia
½ cup cashew cream, unsweetened

Directions
Boil water in a large cooking pot. Add quinoa and cook for 15 minutes. In a separate pan boil milk and add it to cooked quinoa. At the end add cashew cream and stevia.
Mix it and pour in a serving bowl. Refrigerate for few hours then serve.

Nutritional Facts Per Serving:
Calories: 280, Fat: 7 g, Carbs: 24 g, Protein: 10 g, Fiber:8g

DAY 20

Breakfast: Coconut brown rice dressed in avocado cream

Preparation time: 15 minutes
Cooking time: 20 minutes
Servings: 2

Ingredients
Coconut oil to roast
1 tablespoon of roasted pine nuts
1 celery stalk
1/2 cup of black beans (rinsed and drained)
1 orange sweet potato
1-1/2 cup of coconut crème
1-1/2 cups of water
2 cups of brown rice

Avocado cream ingredients
Paprika
Pepper and salt to taste
Dash of quality olive oil
20mm grated ginger
2 tablespoon of coconut cream
Juice of 1/2 lemon
1 avocado

Directions for preparing the avocado cream
Blend together the coconut cream, ginger, lemon juice and avocado in a blender till the cream smoothens. As you blend, add olive oil sparingly. Keep scraping off the blender sides till you arrive at the desired consistency. Add the seasoning of pepper and salt. Best served chilled.

Directions for preparing brown rice
Roast the cube-shaped sweet potatoes in coconut oil until they soften.
In a pot, put in the presoaked brown rice and include the coconut cream and water. Bring the content to boil. When it boils, reduce the heat. Let it cook in a low heat or simmer. Keep watch to keep it from burning. Let the rice take in all the water and don't rinse off. If you prefer, make use of a rice cooker. Slightly roast the pine nuts and chop the deveined celery.
When cooked, mix in the rice with the celery and beans in a bowl, and add salt for seasoning. Include the avocado crème, roasted potatoes topping with the pine nuts.

Nutritional Facts Per Serving:
Calories: 360, Fat: 7 g, Carbs: 42 g, Protein: 8 g, Fiber:12 g

Lunch: Spinach and Mashed Tofu Salad

Preparation time: 10 minutes + 1 hour
Servings: 4

Ingredients:
2,8 oz. blocks firm tofu, drained
4 cups baby spinach leaves
4 tablespoons cashew butter
1½ tablespoon soy sauce
1 inch piece ginger, finely chopped
1 teaspoon red miso paste
2 tablespoons sesame seeds
1 teaspoon organic orange zest
1 teaspoon nori flakes
2 tablespoons water

Directions
Use paper towels to absorb any excess water left in the tofu before crumbling both blocks into small pieces. In a large bowl, combine the mashed tofu with the spinach leaves.
Mix the remaining ingredients in another small bowl and, if desired, add the optional water for a more smooth dressing.
Pour this dressing over the mashed tofu and spinach leaves.
Transfer the bowl to the fridge and allow the salad to chill for up to one hour. Doing so will guarantee a better flavor.
The salad can be served right away. Enjoy!

Nutritional Facts Per Serving:
Calories: 450, Fat: 9 g, Carbs: 30 g, Protein: 21 g, Fiber: 12 g

Dinner: Black Bean and Corn Salad

Preparation time: 10 minutes
Servings: 8

Ingredients

2 cans (15 ounces each) black beans, drained, rinsed
½ cup red onion, finely chopped
1 red bell pepper, chopped
1 yellow bell pepper, chopped
2 cups fresh corn kernels
1 large avocado, peeled, pitted, chopped
2 small tomatoes, chopped
½ cup fresh cilantro, chopped (optional)
4 scallions, chopped
Salt to taste
Pepper to taste
Juice of 2 limes
2 teaspoons dried basil
2 teaspoons dried oregano
1 teaspoon ground cumin

Directions

Add all the ingredients into a bowl and toss well.
Cover and set aside for a while for the flavors to set in.

Nutritional Facts Per Serving:

Calories: 270, Fat: 8 g, Carbs: 25 g, Protein: 12 g, Fiber:20 g

Dessert: Cherry Soft-Serve Ice Cream

Preparation time: 15 minutes
Servings: 3

Ingredients
4 bananas, ripped
1-1/2 cups cherries, frozen and organic
1/4 teaspoon of pure vanilla extract
1/4 cup almond milk
4 tablespoons of vegan chocolate chips

Directions
Dump all the listed ingredients in a food processor.
Pulse it for a few seconds.
Pour the mixture into a serving bowl and refrigerate for a few minutes.
Soft served ice-cream is ready to be devoured.

Nutritional Facts Per Serving:
Calories: 240, Fat: 8 g, Carbs: 30 g, Protein: 10 g, Fiber:2 g

DAY 21

Breakfast: Buckwheat and coconut porridge with blueberry sauce

Preparation time: 5 minutes
Servings: 2

Ingredients For The Porridge
1/2 teaspoon of vanilla essence
1/2 teaspoon of cinnamon
2 tablespoons of coconut oil
2 dates or alternatively 2 tablespoons of rice malt syrup
1/2 cup of coconut milk
1-1/2 cups of buckwheat (soaked and rinsed)

Ingredients for the blueberry sauce
4 tablespoons of coconut water or natural water
1 tablespoon of rice malt syrup
1 cup of blueberries (unfrozen) Ingredients for topping
1 banana
Roasted coconut flakes

Directions
Put together all the ingredients for making the porridge and blend. When it smoothens, transfer into a bowl.
In a clean blender, blend together the ingredients for the blueberry sauce.
Make it easier to blend by adding in some water but don't put too much water.
With a spoon swirl the blueberry sauce on to the porridge.
Include your toppings.

Nutritional Facts Per Serving:
Calories: 270, Fat:4 g, Carbs: 35 g, Protein: 4 g, Fiber:2 g

Lunch: Cucumber Edamame Salad

Preparation time: 5 minutes+ 30 minutes
Cooking time: 8 minutes
Servings: 2

Ingredients
3 tablespoons avocado oil
1 cup cucumber, sliced into thin rounds
½ cup fresh sugar snap peas, sliced or whole
½ cup fresh edamame
¼ cup radish, sliced
1 large Hass avocado, peeled, pitted, sliced
1 nori sheet, crumbled
2 teaspoons roasted sesame seeds
1 teaspoon salt

Directions
Bring a medium-sized pot filled halfway with water to a boil over medium-high heat. Add the sugar snaps and cook them for about 2 minutes.
Take the pot off the heat, drain the excess water, transfer the sugar snaps to a medium-sized bowl and set aside for now.
Fill the pot with water again, add the teaspoon of salt and bring to a boil over medium-high heat. Add the edamame to the pot and let them cook for about 6 minutes.
Take the pot off the heat, drain the excess water, transfer the soybeans to the bowl with sugar snaps and let them cool down for about 5 minutes.
Combine all ingredients, except the nori crumbs and roasted sesame seeds, in a medium-sized bowl. Carefully stir, using a spoon, until all ingredients are evenly coated in oil.
Top the salad with the nori crumbs and roasted sesame seeds. Transfer the bowl to the fridge and allow the salad to cool for at least 30 minutes. Serve chilled and enjoy!

Nutritional Facts Per Serving:
Calories: 320, Fat: 7 g, Carbs: 28 g, Protein: 9 g, Fiber:22 g

Dinner: Tempeh Burgers

Preparation time: 15 minutes
Cooking time: 10 minutes
Servings: 2

Ingredients
1 package (8 ounces) tempeh
For marinade
1 tablespoon sake or white wine
½ tablespoon grated fresh ginger
A pinch red pepper flakes
2 tablespoons soy sauce or tamari
2 tablespoons pineapple juice
1 clove garlic, peeled, minced
¼ teaspoon white pepper

Directions
Make 2 equal slices of the tempeh. Add all the ingredients for marinade into a bowl and whisk well. Place tempeh in it for 15 minutes. Turn once after 10 minutes of marinating.
Preheat the grill to medium-high temperature. Grease the grilling rack with a little oil.
Take out the tempeh from the marinating mixture and place on the grill. Grill for about 4 to 5 minutes on each side. Serve hot over buns and toppings of your choice.

Nutritional Facts Per Serving without bun or toppings
Calories: 320, Fat: 7 g, Carbs: 30 g, Protein: 22 g, Fiber:10 g

Dessert: Pumpkin Oatmeal Muffins

Preparation time: 10 minutes
Cooking time: 28 minutes
Servings: 4

Ingredients
½ cup cooked pumpkin
3 ripe bananas, mashed
½ cup unsweetened applesauce
1 cup rolled oats
1 tablespoon ground flaxseed meal
1 teaspoon pumpkin pie spice
¼ teaspoon of cinnamon
1 teaspoon of baking powder
1 teaspoon pure vanilla extract

Directions
Preheat the oven to 375 degrees F. Line a muffin tray with parchment paper.
Take a bowl and mix all the ingredients. Divide this batter amongst the muffin cups.
Bake in the oven for 28 minutes.
Once, it's golden brown on the top remove from the oven.
Serve and enjoy.

Nutritional Facts Per Serving:
Calories: 240, Fat: 3 g, Carbs: 22 g, Protein: 4 g, Fiber: 6 g

DAY 22

Breakfast: Buckwheat and hempseed pancakes

Preparation time: 10 minutes
Cooking time: 25 minutes
Servings: 1

Ingredients For the ginger-lemon syrup
1 tablespoon of lemon zest
1-inch ginger
1 cup of maple syrup

Ingredients for making the pancake
Coconut oil for cooking
1-1/2 teaspoons of vanilla extract
A pinch teaspoon of salt
1/4 teaspoon of baking soda
1-1/2 teaspoons of baking powder
2 tablespoons of ground flax seeds
3 tablespoons of hemp seeds
4 medjool dates
1 cup of nondairy milk of your choice
1 cup of raw buckwheat groats

Directions for pancakes
Soak the buckwheat groats in water and make sure the water covers them entirely and rises above them by a few millimeters. Squeeze in lemon juice and let them sit overnight.
Strain off the water and rinse off the groats. Let the water drain off completely. If you are using dry dates, let them soften in hot water for some time and drain the water off.
Over medium heat, preheat a non stick skillet. In a high-speed blender process together with all the ingredients till they smoothen. On the sauce pan, put a half teaspoon of the coconut oil. Pour on the mixture right from the blender. Use two tablespoons for each.
When the edges start detaching and the top bubbles, flip the pancake to cook the on the other side. Repeat the same procedure for all the pancakes. The pancakes will have a dark appearance. As you cook put the pancakes on a dinner plate in a warm oven of 200f.

Directions for preparing the lemon ginger syrup
In a pot, put the lemon zest, slices of ginger and the maple syrup. Let them cook over low heat for five minutes. Turn down the heat and leave it for ten minutes. Strain the syrup.

Nutritional Facts Per Serving:
Calories: 330, Fat: 8 g, Carbs: 40 g, Protein: 9 g, Fiber:6 g

Lunch: Artichoke White Bean Sandwich Spread

Preparation time: 10 minutes
Cooking time: 15 minutes
Servings: 2

Ingredients

½ cup raw cashews, chopped
Water
1 clove garlic, cut into half
1 tablespoon lemon zest
1 teaspoon fresh rosemary, chopped
¼ teaspoon salt
¼ teaspoon pepper
6 tablespoons almond, soy or coconut milk
1 15.5-ounce can cannellini beans, rinsed and drained well
3 to 4 canned artichoke hearts, chopped
¼ cup hulled sunflower seeds
Green onions, chopped, for garnish

Directions

Soak the raw cashews for 15 minutes in enough water to cover them. Drain and dab with a paper towel to make them as dry as possible.
Transfer the cashews to a blender and add the garlic, lemon zest, rosemary, salt and pepper. Pulse to break everything up and then add the milk, one tablespoon at a time, until the mixture is smooth and creamy.
Mash the beans in a bowl with a fork. Add the artichoke hearts and sunflower seeds. Toss to mix. Pour the cashew mixture on top and season with more salt and pepper if desired.
Mix the ingredients well and spread on whole-wheat bread, crackers, or a wrap.

Nutritional Facts Per Serving:

Calories: 240, Fat: 4 g, Carbs: 30 g, Protein: 12 g, Fiber:16 g

Dinner: Edamame Salad

Preparation time: 15 minutes
Servings: 4

Ingredients
½ pound frozen edamame, shelled, cooked according to the instructions on the package, drained, rinsed
½ red bell pepper, deseeded, chopped
1-½ cups frozen corn kernels
1 cup red onions, sliced
2 green onions, sliced
1 tablespoon chopped fresh oregano or basil
2 tablespoons chopped parsley

Ingredients For dressing:
3 tablespoons lemon juice
1 tablespoon olive oil
1 tablespoon Dijon mustard
Salt and Pepper to taste

Directions:
To make the dressing whisk together all the ingredients of the dressing.
Add all of the ingredients to a large bowl and toss well. Pour dressing on top.
Toss well. Chill until use.

Nutritional Facts Per Serving:
Calories: 280, Fat: 5 g, Carbs: 18 g, Protein: 16 g, Fiber:20 g

Dessert: Easy Brownies

Preparation time: 10 minutes
Cooking time: 15 minutes
Servings: 8

Ingredients
3 cups of dates, pitted, soft and fresh
1 cup of warm water
1 cup peanut butter
6 tablespoons of coconut oil
1 cup of cocoa powder
1 cup raw walnuts, roughly chopped

Directions
Preheat oven at 375 degrees F. Line a loaf pan with parchment paper. Now, in a food processor blend dates. Take out the dates into a bowl using a spoon. Add hot water to blender and blender until a paste is formed. Add peanut butter, walnuts, coconut oil, and cacao powder to the blender and pulse for few more minutes.
Layer a parchment paper on top. Bake it in the oven for 15 minutes. Then remove from the oven and carefully lift out using edges of parchment paper.
Let it cool for 20 minutes. Enjoy warm or cooled.

Nutritional Facts Per Serving:
Calories: 310, Fat: 10 g, Carbs: 40 g, Protein: 10 g, Fiber:5 g

DAY 23

Breakfast: Protein pancakes
Preparation time: 15 minutes
Cooking time: 10 minutes
Servings: 1

Ingredients
Cooking coconut oil
A pinch of sea salt
1 teaspoon of melted coconut oil
1/2 cup of almond milk
1 teaspoon of baking powder
1 mashed banana
1 scoop of vegan protein powder

Directions
In a bowl put together the milk, melted coconut oil and mashed banana and mix.
Include the salt and baking powder in the mixture.
Mix in the protein powder as you keep stirring until you arrive at a desirable consistency.
Melt the coconut oil in a non-sticky pan over low heat.
When well heated, spread a thin layer of the mixture on the surface and cook till it bubbles on the surface. Flip over when cooked and cook the other side until it is well done.
Do so for the remaining mixture.
You can include your favorite toppings as you serve.

Nutritional Facts Per Serving:
Calories: 310, Fat: 7 g, Carbs: 30 g, Protein: 16 g, Fiber:8 g

Lunch: Buffalo Chickpea Wraps

Preparation time: 20 minutes
Cooking time: 5 minutes
Servings: 4

Ingredients
¼ cup plus 2 tablespoons hummus
2 tablespoons lemon juice
1½ tablespoons maple syrup
1 to 2 tablespoons hot water
1 head Romaine lettuce, chopped
1 15-ounce can chickpeas, drained, rinsed and patted dry
4 tablespoons hot sauce, divided
1 tablespoon olive or coconut oil
¼ teaspoon garlic powder
1 pinch sea salt
4 wheat tortillas
¼ cup cherry tomatoes, diced
¼ cup red onion, diced
¼ of a ripe avocado, thinly sliced

Directions
Mix the hummus with the lemon juice and maple syrup in a large bowl. Use a whisk and add the hot water, a little at a time until it is thick but spreadable.
Add the Romaine lettuce and toss to coat. Set aside.
Pour the prepared chickpeas into another bowl. Add three tablespoons of the hot sauce, the olive oil, garlic powder and salt; toss to coat.
Heat a metal skillet (cast iron works the best) over medium heat and add the chickpea mixture. Sauté for three to five minutes and mash gently with a spoon.
Once the chickpea mixture is slightly dried out, remove from the heat and add the rest of the hot sauce. Stir it in well and set aside.
Lay the tortillas on a clean, flat surface and spread a quarter cup of the buffalo chickpeas on top. Top with tomatoes, onion and avocado (optional) and wrap.

Nutritional Facts Per Serving:
Calories: 350, Fat: 9 g, Carbs: 32 g, Protein: 16 g, Fiber:19 g

Dinner: Zucchini Sandwich with Balsamic Dressing

Preparation time: 5 minutes
Cooking time: 2 minutes
Servings: 2

Ingredients
2 small zucchinis
1 tablespoon olive oil
4 cloves garlic, thinly sliced
1 tablespoon balsamic vinegar
1 large roasted red pepper, chopped
1 cup cannellini beans, rinsed, drained
2 whole-wheat sandwich rolls
6 to 8 basil leaves
½ teaspoon pepper

Directions
Add the oil to a hot skillet and sauté the garlic for one or two minutes or until it just starts to brown.
Add the zucchini strips and sauté in batches (don't overcrowd) and lay out on a plate until they are all finished.
Reduce heat to medium and place all the zucchini strips back in the pan.
Add the vinegar and sauté for about a minute.
In the blender, process the red pepper and beans until smooth.
Toast the buns and spoon onto the bottom halves the bean and pepper mixture.
Lay basil leaves on top and then the zucchini.
Grind some pepper on top and close the sandwich with the top of the bun.

Nutritional Facts Per Serving:
Calories: 290, Fat: 6 g, Carbs: 29 g, Protein: 11 g, Fiber:9 g

Dessert: Homemade Chocolate Ice-Cream

Preparation time: 10 minutes
Servings: 6

Ingredients
3 cups raw cashew, pre-soaked and drained
3 cups almond milk, unsweetened
6 tablespoons cacao powder, organic
Salt, pinch
4 scoops of stevia

Directions
In a high-speed blender, pulse all the ingredients
Transfer this mixture to the plastic container.
Refrigerate for 6 hours.
Once solid, serve and enjoy.

Nutritional Facts Per Serving:
Calories: 280, Fat: 10 g, Carbs: 30 g, Protein: 9 g, Fiber:2 g

DAY 24

Breakfast: Quinoa and oats focaccia bread
Preparation time: 10 minutes
Cooking time: 20 minutes
Servings: 2

Ingredients
1/4 cup of olive oil
1/2 cup of quinoa flakes
1/2 cup of oat flour
2 cups of gluten free wheat flour
1 tablespoon of psyllium husk
1 teaspoon of sea salt
1 tablespoon of maple syrup
5 teaspoons of active dry yeast
2 cups of luke warm water

Directions
In the warm water, let the yeast dissolve. In the dissolved yeast, include the psyllium, maple syrup, and salt and combine.
Mix in the quinoa flakes and the flours and stir well. Add the oil into the mixture and combine once again. Leave the mixture covered in a dump cloth through the night.
The following morning put the dough into a baking tray and brush on some oil.
Preheat your oven to 350f. Oil and flour your hands and do the flour in to the desired focaccia shape, making it thin. Leave the bread to rise and make some holes in it. Put generous amounts of oil into the holes.
Include rosemary, and cherry tomatoes on top and let it bake for twenty minutes till it turns golden brown on the surface.

Nutritional Facts Per Serving:
Calories: 380, Fat: 8 g, Carbs: 40 g, Protein: 6 g, Fiber:4 g

Lunch: Coconut Veggie Wraps

Preparation time: 15 minutes
Servings: 5

Ingredients
1½ cups shredded carrots
1 red bell pepper, seeded, thinly sliced
2½ cups kale
1 ripe avocado, thinly sliced
1 cup fresh cilantro, chopped (optional)
5 coconut wraps
2/3 cups hummus
6½ cups green curry paste

Directions
Slice, chop and shred all the vegetables.
Lay a coconut wrap on a clean flat surface and spread two tablespoons of the hummus and one tablespoon of the green curry paste on top of the end closest to you.
Place some carrots, bell pepper, kale and cilantro on the wrap and start rolling it up, starting from the edge closest to you. Roll tightly and fold in the ends. Place the wrap, seam down, on a plate to serve.

Nutritional Facts Per Serving:
Calories: 190, Fat: 3 g, Carbs: 20 g, Protein: 12 g, Fiber: 14 g

Dinner: Delicious Sloppy Joes With No Meat

Preparation time: 15 minutes
Cooking time: 35/40 minutes
Servings: 4

Ingredients

5 tablespoons vegetable stock
2 stalks celery, diced
1 small onion, diced
1 small red bell pepper, diced
1 teaspoon garlic powder
1 teaspoon chili powder
1 teaspoon ground cumin
1 teaspoon salt
1 cup cooked bulgur wheat
1 cup red lentils
1 15-ounce can tomato sauce
4 tablespoons tomato paste
3½ cups water
2 teaspoons balsamic vinegar
1 tablespoon Hoisin sauce

Directions

In a Dutch oven, heat up the vegetable stock and add the celery, onion and bell pepper. Sauté until vegetables are soft, about five minutes. Add the garlic powder, chili powder, cumin and salt and mix in. Add the bulgur wheat, lentils, tomato sauce, tomato paste, water, vinegar and Hoisin sauce. Stir and bring to a boil.

Turn the heat down to a simmer and cook uncovered for 30 minutes. Stir occasionally to prevent sticking and scorching.

Taste to see if the lentils are tender. When the lentils are done, serve on buns.

Nutritional Facts Per Serving:

Calories: 450, Fat: 9 g, Carbs: 42 g, Protein: 16 g, Fiber:12 g

Dessert: Dessert Time Parfait

Preparation time: 5 minutes+ 2 hours
Servings: 3

Ingredients
1 cup of coconut yogurt
1 cup berries
1 cup bananas, peeled and chopped
1 cup apples, chopped
1 cup Granola
1 cup almonds, chopped

Directions
Take a bowl, and layer granola, then yogurt followed by fruits, and almonds. Repeat this step twice and then refrigerate for a few hours.
Once it's done, serve.

Nutritional Facts Per Serving:
Calories: 280, Fat: 10 g, Carbs: 32 g, Protein: 12 g, Fiber:6 g

DAY 25

Breakfast: Sweet molasses bread
Preparation time: 20 minutes+ 2 hours
Cooking time: 30 minutes
Servings: 4

Ingredients
Old fashioned rolled oats 1-1/2 teaspoon of instant yeast
1-1/4 teaspoon of salt
1/2 teaspoon of ground nutmeg
2 tablespoons of brown sugar
3 tablespoons of unsweetened cocoa powder
2-2/3 cups of white whole wheat flour
3 cups of all purpose wheat flour
4 tablespoons of coconut oil or nondairy butter
1/2 cup of molasses
Three half cups of warm non dairy milk or almond milk

Directions
Put together all the dry ingredients plus the yeast and combine them.
Using a wooden spoon, mix in the butter, molasses, and milk. When mixed in, use your hand side to knee the mixture to a smoother texture.
Covered in a kitchen clothe, let the dough rise in a warm place for about 60 minutes.
Dust a flat surface and places the dough on it. Split it into three equal portions and give them the shape of bread. Place the dough pieces in greased baking tins, or greased baking sheets. Alternatively, use a parchment lined baking sheet. Sprinkle on oats and leave it to rise while covered for another 60 minutes. As it rises, preheat your oven to 350f. Cook for 30 minutes and test if it is well done using a toothpick or a tester. The color should deepen when cooled.
Remove the pieces of cooked bread and place them on a rack to let them cool. You can have them cooled or while still warm.

Nutritional Facts Per Serving:
Calories: 340, Fat: 9 g, Carbs: 40 g, Protein: 9 g, Fiber:10 g

Lunch: Cucumber Avocado Sandwich

Preparation time: 15 minutes
Servings: 2

Ingredients:
½ of a large cucumber, peeled, sliced
¼ teaspoon salt
4 slices whole-wheat bread
4 ounces goat cheese with or without herbs, at room temperature
2 Romaine lettuce leaves
1 large avocado, peeled, pitted, sliced
2 pinches lemon pepper
1 squeeze of lemon juice
½ cup alfalfa sprouts

Directions
Peel and slice the cucumber thinly. Lay the slices on a plate and sprinkle them with a quarter to a half teaspoon of salt. Let this set for 10 minutes or until water appears on the plate.
Place the cucumber slices in a colander and rinse with cold water. Let these drain, then place them on a dry plate and pat dry with a paper towel. Spread all slices with goat cheese and place lettuce leaves on the two bottom pieces of bread.
Layer the cucumber slices and avocado atop the bread. Sprinkle one pinch of lemon pepper over each sandwich and drizzle a little lemon juice over the top.
Top with the alfalfa sprouts and place another piece of bread, goat cheese down, on top.

Nutritional Facts Per Serving:
Calories: 280, Fat: 10 g, Carbs: 26 g, Protein: 9 g, Fiber:12 g

Dinner: Ricotta Basil Pinwheels

Preparation time: 10 minutes+ 30 minutes
Servings: 4

Ingredients
½ cup unsalted cashews
Water
7 ounces firm tofu, cut into pieces
¼ cup almond milk
1 teaspoon white wine vinegar
1 clove garlic, smashed
20 to 25 fresh basil leaves
Salt and pepper to taste
8 tortillas
7 ounces fresh spinach
½ cup black olives, sliced
2 to 3 tomatoes, cut into small pieces

Directions
Soak the cashews for 30 minutes in enough water to cover them. Drain them well and pat them dry with paper towels. Place the cashews in a blender along with the tofu, almond milk, vinegar, garlic, basil leaves, salt and pepper to taste. Blend until smooth and creamy.
Spread the resulting mixture on the eight tortillas, dividing it equally. Top with spinach leaves, olives and tomatoes. Tightly roll each loaded tortilla.
Cut off the ends with a sharp knife and slice into four or five pinwheels.

Nutritional Facts Per Serving:
Calories: 340, Fat: 12 g, Carbs: 22 g, Protein: 16 g, Fiber:9 g

Dessert: Applesauce Muffins

Preparation time: 10 minutes
Cooking time: 25 minutes
Servings: 12

Ingredients
2 cups whole wheat flour
1 teaspoon baking powder
½ teaspoon ground allspice
½ cup brown sugar
15 ounces apple sauce
½ cup almond milk
1 teaspoon vanilla
1 teaspoon apple cider vinegar
½ cup raisins
½ cup apple, diced

Directions
Preheat your oven to 350 degrees F. Separately, whisk together the dry ingredients in one bowl and wet ingredients in another bowl. Beat the two mixture together until smooth. Fold in apples and raisins, give it a gentle stir.
Line a muffin tray with muffin cups and evenly divide the muffin batter among the cups.
Bake for nearly 25 minutes and serve.

Nutritional Facts Per Serving:
Calories: 220, Fat: 4 g, Carbs: 35 g, Protein: 8 g, Fiber:10 g

DAY 26

Breakfast: Chocolate Peanut Butter Shake
Preparation time: 6 minutes
Servings: 4

Ingredients
4 bananas, peeled
2 tablespoons of cacao powder
4 tablespoons of peanut butter
1 cup of almond milk

Directions
Combine all the listed ingredients in a blender and pulse until smooth. Pour into tall serving glasses and enjoy.

Nutritional Facts Per Serving:
Calories: 320, Fat: 10 g, Carbs: 32 g, Protein: 10 g, Fiber:2 g

Lunch: Lentil Sandwich Spread

Preparation time: 15 minutes
Cooking time: 20 minutes
Servings: 3

Ingredients
1 tablespoon water or oil
1 small onion, chopped
2 cloves garlic, minced
1 cup dry lentils
2 cups vegetable stock
1 tablespoon apple cider vinegar
2 tablespoons tomato paste
3 sun-dried tomatoes
2 tablespoons maple
1 teaspoon dried oregano
½ teaspoon ground cumin
1 teaspoon coriander
1 teaspoon turmeric
½ lemon, juiced
1 tablespoon fresh parsley, chopped

Directions
Warm a Dutch oven over medium heat and add the water or oil.
Immediately add the onions and sauté for two to three minutes or until softened. Add more water if this starts to stick to the pan. Add the garlic and sauté for one minute.
Add the lentils, vegetable stock and vinegar; bring to a boil. Turn down to a simmer and cook for 15 minutes or until the lentils are soft and the liquid is almost completely absorbed.
Ladle the lentils into a food processor and add the tomato paste, sun-dried tomatoes and syrup; process until smooth. Add the oregano, cumin, coriander, turmeric and lemon; processes until thoroughly mixed.
Remove the spread to a bowl and apply it to bread, toast, a wrap, or pita. Sprinkle with toppings as desired.

Nutritional Facts Per Serving:
Calories: 380, Fat: 6 g, Carbs: 40 g, Protein: 10 g, Fiber16 g

Dinner: Sweet Potato Sandwich Spread

Preparation time: 10 minutes
Cooking time: 18/20 minutes
Servings: 4

Ingredients
1 large sweet potato baked, peeled
1 teaspoon cumin
1 teaspoon chili powder
1 teaspoon garlic powder
Salt and pepper to taste
2 slices whole-wheat bread
1 to 2 tablespoons pinto beans, drained
Lettuce

Directions
Bake and peel the sweet potato and mash it in a bowl. If it is too thick, add a little almond or coconut milk.
Mix in the cumin, chili powder, garlic powder, salt and pepper.
Spread the mixture on a slice of bread and spoon some beans on top.
Top with lettuce leaves and the other slice of bread.

Nutritional Facts Per Serving:
Calories: 280, Fat: 4 g, Carbs: 32 g, Protein: 6 g, Fiber:9 g

Dessert: Keto Vanilla Pannacotta

Preparation time: 15 minutes + 2 hours
Cooking time: 5 minutes
Servings: 2

Ingredients
1 teaspoon gelatin powder
1 cup of water, for mixing
2 cups heavy whipping cream
1 tablespoon vanilla extract
1 pomegranate, seeds

Directions
Pour water in a bowl, and soak the gelatin powder in it.
Let it sit for 5 minutes.
Next, take a pan, and add vanilla extract and cream in it.
Simmer the mixture for a few minutes.
Once the cream gets thick, add gelatin.
Mix well and then turn off the flame.
Pour the cream into serving bowls.
Refrigerate it for 2 hours.
Once it's solid, serve with the topping of pomegranate seeds.
Enjoy.

Nutritional Facts Per Serving:
Calories: 380, Fat: 28 g, Carbs: 20 g, Protein: 10 g, Fiber:1 g

DAY 27

Breakfast: Berries Smoothie

Preparation time: 5 minutes
Servings: 2

Ingredients
1 cup raspberries
½ cup strawberries
½ cup blueberries
1 cup almond milk
½ inch ginger cube
Pinch of salt
Pinch of black pepper

Directions
Pulse all the ingredients in a blender until a smooth consistency is formed. Pour into ice-filled serving glasses and enjoy.

Nutritional Facts Per Serving:
Calories: 210, Fat: 2 g, Carbs: 20 g, Protein: 4 g, Fiber:12 g

Lunch: Rice and Bean Burritos

Preparation time: 10 minutes
Cooking time: 15 minutes
Servings: 8

Ingredients
2 16-ounce cans fat-free refried beans
6 tortillas
2 cups cooked rice
½ cup salsa
1 tablespoon olive oil
1 bunch green onions, chopped
2 bell peppers, finely chopped
Guacamole

Directions
Preheat the oven to 375°F.
Dump the refried beans into a saucepan and place over medium heat to warm.
Heat the tortillas and lay them out on a flat surface.
Spoon the beans in a long mound that runs across the tortilla, just a little off from center.
Spoon some rice and salsa over the beans; add the green pepper and onions to taste, along with any other finely chopped vegetables you like.
Fold over the shortest edge of the plain tortilla and roll it up, folding in the sides as you go.
Place each burrito, seam side down, on a nonstick-sprayed baking sheet.
Brush with olive oil and bake for 15 minutes.
Serve with guacamole.

Nutritional Facts Per Serving:
Calories: 300, Fat: 8 g, Carbs: 30 g, Protein: 14 g, Fiber: 9 g

Dinner: Mediterranean Tortilla Pinwheels

Preparation time: 15 minutes
Servings: 6

Ingredients
½ cup water
4 tablespoons white vinegar
3 tablespoons lemon juice
3 tablespoons tahini paste
1 clove garlic, minced
Salt and pepper to taste
Canned artichokes, drained, thinly sliced
Cherry tomatoes, thinly sliced
Olives, thinly sliced
Lettuce or baby spinach
Tortillas

Directions
In a bowl, combine the water, vinegar, lemon juice and Tahini paste; whisk together until smooth. Add the garlic, salt and pepper to taste; whisk to combine. Set the bowl aside.
Lay a tortilla on a flat surface and spread with one tablespoon of the sauce. Lay some lettuce or spinach slices on top, then scatter some artichoke, tomato and olive slices on top.
Tightly roll the tortilla and fold in the sides. Cut the ends off and then slice into four or five pinwheels.

Nutritional Facts Per Serving:
Calories: 320, Fat: 6 g, Carbs: 35 g, Protein: 8 g, Fiber:10 g

Dessert: Apple Pie Bites

Preparation time: 10 minutes+ 1 hour
Servings: 12

Ingredients
1 cup walnuts, chopped
½ cup coconut oil
¼ cup ground flax seeds
½ ounce freeze dried apples
1 teaspoon vanilla extract
1 teaspoon cinnamon
Liquid stevia, to taste

Directions
In a bowl add all the ingredients.
Mix well then roll the mixture into small balls.
Freeze them for 1 hour to set.
Serve.

Nutritional Facts Per Serving:
Calories: 190, Fat: 3 g, Carbs: 30 g, Protein: 6 g, Fiber:4 g

DAY 28

Breakfast: Sunrise Smoothie

Preparation time: 5 minutes
Servings: 2

Ingredients
1 cup unsweetened almond milk
1 cup oranges, peeled and seedless
1 cup of pomegranate
2 medium bananas
1 cup unsweetened strawberries
2 tablespoons chia seed

Directions
Dump all the ingredients in a blender and pulse for few minutes.
Once smooth inconsistency.
Pour into ice-filled serving glasses and enjoy.

Nutritional Facts Per Serving:
Calories: 150, Fat: 2 g, Carbs: 17 g, Protein: 4 g, Fiber:10 g

Lunch: Sun-dried Tomato Spread

Preparation time: 40 minutes + 8 hours
Servings: 8

Ingredients
1 cup sun-dried tomatoes
1 cup raw cashews
Water for soaking tomatoes and cashews
½ cup water
1 clove garlic, minced
1 green onion, chopped
5 large basil leaves
½ teaspoon lemon juice
¼ teaspoon salt
1 dash pepper
Hulled sunflower seeds

Directions
Soak tomatoes and cashews for 30 minutes in separate bowls, with enough water to cover them. Drain and pat dry. Put the tomatoes and cashews in a food processor and puree them, drizzling the water in as it purees to make a smooth, creamy paste. Add the garlic, onion, basil leaves, lemon juice, salt and pepper and mix thoroughly.
Scrape into a bowl, cover and refrigerate overnight.
Spread on bread or toast and sprinkle with sunflower seeds for a little added crunch.

Nutritional Facts Per Serving:
Calories: 200, Fat: 8 g, Carbs: 28 g, Protein: 10 g, Fiber: 12 g

Dinner: Spicy Hummus and Apple Wrap

Preparation time: 20 minutes
Servings: 1

Ingredients
3 to 4 tablespoons hummus
2 tablespoons mild salsa
½ cup broccoli slaw
½ teaspoon fresh lemon juice
2 teaspoons plain yogurt
salt and pepper to taste
1 tortilla
Lettuce leaves
½ Granny Smith or another tart apple, cored and thinly sliced

Directions
In a small bowl, mix the hummus with the salsa. Set the bowl aside.
In a large bowl, mix the broccoli slaw, lemon juice and yogurt. Season with the salt and pepper.
Lay the tortilla on a flat surface and spread on the hummus mixture.
Lay down some lettuce leaves on top of the hummus.
On the upper half of the tortilla, place a pile of the broccoli slaw mixture and cover with the apples. Fold and wrap.

Nutritional Facts Per Serving:
Calories: 310, Fat: 9 g, Carbs: 30 g, Protein: 16 g, Fiber:12 g

Dessert: Cinnamon Spiced Apples

Preparation time: 10 minutes
Cooking time: 4 hours
Servings: 4

Ingredients
1/3 cup sugar
1/4 cup packed brown sugar
1 tablespoon cornstarch
3 teaspoons ground cinnamon
1/8 teaspoon ground nutmeg
6 large Granny Smith apples, peeled and cut into eighths
1/4 cup nondairy butter, cubed
6 scoops of vegan ice-cream

Directions
Take a large mixing bowl, and mix the first five ingredients in it.
Place the mixture into a slow cooker.
Add apples to the cooker.
Top it with butter and cover the slow cooker.
Cook for 4 hours until apples are tender.
Serve with vegan ice-cream.

Nutritional Facts Per Serving:
Calories: 280, Fat: 6 g, Carbs: 24 g, Protein: 5 g, Fiber: 16 g

Shopping list

Week 1: Shopping List

2 packages of vegetable stock	1 orange
11 carrots	1 papaya
1 package of cayenne pepper	1 yellow bell pepper
2 packages of cilantro	1 package of frozen greens (i.e. spinach, kale)
4 lemons	1 package of mixed frozen berries
2 cans full fat coconut milk	2 sweet onions
3 packages of coconut milk	1 package of broccoli
2 packages of psyllium husk	1 package of nutmeg
1 package of raspberries	1 package of basil
2 kiwis	3 packages of hemp seeds
3 packages of spinach	1 package of coconut flakes (unsweetened)
1 kale	2 packages of rolled oats
24 bananas	2 mangos
1 package of spelt flour	1 can of sweet corn
3 packages of ground flaxseeds	11 red bell peppers
1 package of salt	1 peach
2 packages of cinnamon	2 coconuts
1 package of almonds	3 packages of blueberries
3 package of hazelnuts	1 bottle of lime juice
2 package of walnuts	1 package of thyme
2 packages of pecans	1 package of oregano
1 package of dried fruit (of choice)	1 pineapple
2 packages of vanilla extract	2 packages of coconut flour
1 package of couscous	2 packages of almond flour
1 bottle of maple syrup	1 package of red lentils
1 bottle of olive oil	1 package of bay leaves
3 packages of chickpeas	1 package of chili powder
18 onions	1 package of black pepper
1 package of cumin	2 packages of mushrooms
1 package of turmeric	1 bottle of stevia
2 red peppers	14 tomatoes
8 sweet potatoes	1 package of kidney beans
1 package of ground coriander	2 packages of black beans
1 package of chia seeds	1 package of smoked paprika powder
2 packages of almond milk	1 brown bread
1 package of coconut oil	1 package of green chili flakes
1 ginger root	1 package of coconut butter
1 package of spicy paprika powder	1 package of firm tofu
5 heads of garlic	2 packages of brown rice
1 package of tabasco sauce	1 radish
1 bottle of MCT oil	1 cucumber

1 eggplant	1 package of edamame (shelled)
1 package of tahini	1 package of sesame seeds
1 bottle of flaxseed oil	1 package of cocoa butter
1 packages of baking powder	1 package of vegan protein powder
3 packages of coconut cream	1 package of dried thyme
1 package of cocoa powder	1 package of whole wheat flour
3 packages of tempeh	2 packages of cashews
1 purple cabbage	2 packages of nutritional yeast
2 packages of quinoa	1 package of paprika powder
1 package of soy sauce	1 bottle of red wine
1 bottle of sesame oil	10 potatoes
1 bottle of rice vinegar	2 fresh parsleys
1 package of chili flakes	3 celery stalks
1 package of red curry paste	1 package of miso

Week 2: Shopping List

1 bottle of olive oil	1 package of coriander
3 packages of black beans	1 package of ground turmeric
5 green onions	2 packages of vegetable stock
6 red bell peppers	1 bottle of avocado oil
1 package of mushrooms	1 package of garlic powder
1 package of cumin	1 package of oregano
1 package of tabasco sauce	3 Chioggia beets
1 package of chili powder	2 avocados
1 package of salt	1 package of wasabi powder
1 package of sugar	1 package of sushi rice
2 packages of whole wheat flour	2 packages of edamame beans
1 package of coconut oil	1 package of pecans
1 package of almond butter	1 package of matcha powder
1 package of almond flour	1 package of freeze dried peach powder
4 packages of almond milk	1 eggplant
1 bottle of sesame oil	1 package of tahini
2 packages of tofu (1 extra firm)	1 package of coconut butter
2 packages of baking soda	1 package of sriracha
1 package of sesame seeds	1 package of brown sugar
3 zucchinis	1 package of wasabi paste
1 package of rolled oats	1 package of pickled ginger
1 package of oat milk	2 packages of blueberries
1 package of coconut oil	1 package of strawberries
3 packages of ground flaxseeds	1 package of blackberries
1 package of chia seeds	1 bag (300g) of tortilla chips
1 package of vanilla sticks	4 large tortillas (whole wheat)
1 package of kosher salt	2 green apples
1 package of cinnamon	1 package of sea salt
1 package of psyllium husk	1 package of red pepper flakes
2 cans of full fat coconut milk	1 bottle of cherry vinegar

1 bottle of stevia	1 package of black pepper
5 lemons / 1 lime	1 package of miso
3 packages of raspberries	1 package of rosemary
1 package of almonds	2 packages of baking powder
1 package of coconut flour	1 pumpkin
2 packages of oatmeal	1 package of dark chocolate chips (vegan friendly)
13 bananas	4 jazz apples
2 packages of hemp seeds	4 Red Delicious apples
1 package of lentils	15 oz of tempeh
1 ginger root	1 purple cabbage
9 onions (2 yellow onions)	1 package of broccoli
1 head of garlic	1 package of soy sauce
1 package of tomato paste	1 bottle of rice vinegar
1 package of curry powder	2 packages of cashews
1 package of red hot pepper flakes	1 package of chili flakes
1 jar of diced tomatoes	1 package of red curry paste
1 package of pepper	2 packages of coconut milk
2 cilantros	2 packages of coconut cream
2 packages of spinach	1 kiwi
2 kales	2 apples
14 carrots	1 pineapple
6 celery stalks	1 mango
1 package of nutritional yeast	1 package of couscous
1 package of thyme	1 package of chickpeas
4 fresh parsleys	1 red pepper
1 package of vanilla flavored vegan protein powder	1 package of cayenne pepper
1 dark vegan chocolate	1 package of cilantro
1 bottle of MCT oil	1 package of hazelnut spread
1 package of cocoa powder	1 package of vanilla extract
1 package of brown rice	1 can of sweet corn
1 package of white rice	2 packages of quinoa
1 package of hazelnut	1 tomato
1 green bell pepper	6 sweet potatoes

Week 3: Shopping List

3 packages of tempeh	2 lemons
3 packages of quinoa	1 package of Dijon mustard
7 red bell peppers	1 package of nutritional yeast
1 purple cabbage	1 package of sweet paprika powder
2 sweet potatoes	1 package of nutmeg
1 kale	1 package of asparagus
1 package of broccoli	1 package of peas
1 bottle of sesame oil	1 package of baking soda
1 bottle of soy sauce	1 package of chickpeas
1 bottle of rice vinegar	1 package of spicy paprika powder

1 bottle of stevia	1 package of baby spinach
16 bananas	1 package of oregano
3 packages of coconut milk	1 package of avocado oil
2 packages of blueberries	1 package of garlic powder
2 packages of raspberries	1 bottle of canola oil
2 packages of vanilla extract	1 package of white beans
3 packages of rolled oats	1 package of kidney beans
1 package of walnuts	1 roma tomato
2 packages of chia seeds	1 package of paprika powder
3 packages of black beans	3 fresh cilantros
4 heads of garlic	1 avocado
1 sweet onion	1 package of cilantro
3 green bell peppers	1 ginger root
2 packages of whole wheat flour	3 green onions
2 packages of smoked paprika powder	4 zucchinis
1 package of cumin	1 package of sesame seeds
1 package of salt	1 jar of peanut butter
1 package of pepper	1 package of chili flakes
1 brown bread	1 bottle of maple syrup
6 tortillas (whole wheat)	1 package of almonds
2 packages of brown rice	1 package of pumpkin seeds
2 dark vegan chocolates	1 package of dates
1 package of vanilla flavored vegan protein powder	1 vanilla stick
2 kiwis	1 bottle of agave nectar
2 packages of spinach	3 packages of almond milk
2 packages of ground flaxseeds	1 package of cinnamon
1 pineapple	1 package of cayenne pepper
1 mango	3 jalapeño peppers
1 bottle of flaxseed oil	1 yellow squash
1 bottle of olive oil	1 bottle of tomato paste
3 packages of hemp seeds	2 cans of sweet corn
2 packages of almond flour	1 package of chili powder
3 packages of baking powder	1 coconut
7 red onions	1 bottle of MCT oil
6 sweet red peppers	3 packages of cashews
2 cans (4oz) of green chilis	1 lime
1 package of dry pinto beans	1 package of oat milk
1 package of whole wheat spaghetti	1 package of coconut oil
1 package of tahini	1 package of kosher salt

Week 4: Shopping List

2 packages of brown rice	1 package of coconut oil
1 bottle of olive oil	1 package of tabasco sauce
2 packages of Portobello mushrooms	1 eggplant
3 packages of cashews	1 pineapple
1 package of basil leaves	1 mango

1 bottle of red wine	1 coconut
1 package of nutritional yeast	2 cans (14 oz.) unsweetened coconut milk
1 package of pepper	1 can diced green chilies
11 onions (3 red, 2 white, 1 green, 2 brown)	1 package of curry powder
2 heads of garlic	15 oz. tempeh
4 carrots	1 purple cabbage
7 celery stalks	2 packages of quinoa
8 sweet potatoes	1 package of soy sauce
2 kales	1 package of broccoli
9 bell peppers (1 green, red and yellow)	1 bottle of sesame oil
1 package of thyme	1 bottle of rice vinegar
1 package of miso	1 package of red curry paste
4 fresh parsleys	1 package of garlic powder
1 fresh cilantro	1 package of strawberries
1 package of rosemary	1 package of black berries
1 package of miso	1 zucchini
1 package of peanut butter	1 bottle of white wine vinegar
1 package of cocoa powder	1 package of vegan BBQ sauce
3 packages of coconut flour	1 lime
1 package of vanilla flavored vegan protein powder	1 package of cinnamon
1 package of cumin	1 package of whole wheat flour
1 package of cayenne pepper	1 package of sesame seeds
1 package of tahini	1 package of hemp seeds
3 packages of baking powder	1 package of salt
3 packages of chickpeas	1 bottle of agave nectar
4 green apples	1 package of dates
13 bananas	2 packages of vanilla extract
2 oranges	1 bottle of MCT oil
1 ginger root	1 bottle of stevia
3 lemons	1 package of spinach
2 kiwis	1 ginger root
3 packages of coconut milk	1 cucumber
2 packages of walnuts	3 packages of blueberries
1 package of goji berries	2 packages of raspberries
1 package of pumpkin seeds	1 package of coconut butter
2 packages of rolled oats	2 packages of almond flour
3 packages of almonds	1 package of almonds
1 bottle of agave nectar	1 package of full fat coconut milk
1 package of chia seeds	1 package of freeze dried blueberry powder
1 package of glucomannan powder	1 package of freeze dried apples
1 bottle of flaxseed oil	2 packages of black beans
1 pumpkin	1 package of white beans
1 package of onion powder	2 jalapeños
1 package of bay leaves	4 large tomatoes
1 package of almond butter	1 dark vegan chocolate
2 packages of baking soda	1 package of hazelnuts
1 package of paprika powder	2 packages of coconut cream

Conclusion

I believe now you understand how a plant-based diet lifestyle can be beneficial to you. I hope that the book answered all questions you may have heard about this style of dieting and that you can start to make it work for you. If you are still hesitant about entirely giving up animal products, you don't have to.

The main take away here is that you make plant-based meals the main part of your diet as you make baby steps to transition into a full plant-based lifestyle. You will soon realize that your body and mind start to feel better, stronger and healthier. You can't fix your health until you fix your diet!

The next step is trying out the different recipes outlined in the book. As we have seen in the book, there are many advantages of adapting to plant-based foods. Generally, it is the best way of a healthy life. If you are battling with weight challenges why not try out the low-calorie recipes? You don't have to go fully blown vegan rather every once in a while, killing those meat cravings the right way. Over time you will realize the benefits of eating plant foods.

If you have been through this book you certainly enjoy being in the kitchen. Experiment with different foods and create your own recipes. Check out other recipe books and borrow ideas from them. You don't have to be strict with the directions given in the book; instead create your own from the ideas you attained from this book. As you enjoy the recipes, share them with your family and friends and let every meal tell a tale.

By the same author

Plant-based diet cookbook for beginners

Vegan cookbook with quick & easy everyday recipes for a healthy lifestyle. Wholefood tasty seasonal dishes and simple plant-based meals on a budget.

Plant-based diet for beginners

A complete and easy guide to go on a plant-based diet and never leave it. Reset and energize your body with vegan recipes. Includes a Weekly Plant-Based Meal Plan.

Plant based high-protein cookbook

101 vegan recipes for tasty and healthy high-protein meals. Boost your athletic performance and increase energy. Includes a three-week plan

Lightning Source UK Ltd.
Milton Keynes UK
UKHW050831030621
384857UK00002B/4